The Other Roswell:

UFO Crash
On the Texas-Mexico Border

Noe Torres and Ruben Uriarte

As Told to the Authors By
Colonel Robert B. Willingham,
U.S. Air Force Reserve (Retired)

RoswellBooks.com

Preface

In 1978, nuclear physicist and part-time UFO investigator Stanton Friedman stumbled upon compelling evidence that an unidentified flying object crashed near Roswell, New Mexico in July 1947. While following up on a lead that a retired military officer living in Louisiana had been talking about the incident, Friedman located Jessie Marcel, Sr., who had served as Intelligence Officer at the Roswell Army Air Field when the crash occurred. As a result of Friedman connecting with Marcel in 1978 and his further research into the case, the Roswell UFO crash quickly became the world's most famous flying saucer story.

Before Friedman helped Roswell become a household name, though, at least one civilian UFO investigator was already seriously looking into another highly credible case that also involved the crash of an unidentified flying object. This "other Roswell" is sometimes called *The Del Rio UFO Crash*, because it occurred near Del Rio, a city in Southwest Texas, located on the border with Mexico. A brief account of the incident was first published in a Pennsylvania weekly newspaper in 1967, based on testimony provided by an eyewitness, Robert B. Willingham, a colonel in the United States Air Force Reserve. In 1978, Willingham's story was chosen by Japanese television as one of America's top UFO cases and was featured in a major documentary filmed in Texas and Mexico for Japanese television.

Although Willingham's remarkable story first surfaced more than ten years before Friedman's work on the Roswell case began, nobody followed up on Willingham's account until many years after he first revealed it. Among those who read the 1967 article about Willingham's UFO encounter was a member of a civilian UFO group called the National Investigations Committee on Aerial Phenomena (NICAP). The member clipped the article out of the paper and mailed it to NICAP headquarters in Washington, D.C., where it went into a file folder and remained unread for ten years.

In 1977, another NICAP member, Todd Zechel, found the long-ignored clipping and tracked down the eyewitness, Robert Willingham, who was retired from the military but still living in

Pennsylvania. After many interviews with the retired colonel, Zechel became convinced that Willingham's amazing tale of a UFO crash along the Texas-Mexico border should be told to the world, and he began planning a book. He also participated in the filming of the 1978 Japanese television documentary about the case. When the Roswell, New Mexico, UFO story surfaced two years later in the book *The Roswell Incident*, Zechel remained firmly convinced that Willingham's encounter was at least as important and credible, if not more so.

However, as time went on, the Roswell case seemed to suck away all interest in other UFO crash retrieval cases, and Willingham's eyewitness account of a UFO crash near Del Rio, Texas, slowly receded into the background, never being published as a book, until now. In 2007, while investigating another case, involving a mid-air collision between a UFO and an airplane, the authors ran across bits and pieces of the Willingham story. After completing our book *Mexico's Roswell: The Chihuahua UFO Crash* in March 2007, we began working in earnest on Willingham's intriguing UFO encounter.

With assistance from veteran UFO researcher Dr. Bruce Maccabee and Dallas television reporter Richard Ray, we discovered, to our delight, that Colonel Willingham was still very much alive and residing in a small town near Wichita Falls, Texas. We made initial contact by phone and later visited him at his home. Since then, we have spent many hours talking with him about "the other Roswell," Willingham's eyewitness testimony about the crash of an unidentified flying object near Del Rio.

This is Colonel Willingham's incredible tale, which has been waiting for so long to be told. We remain eternally thankful that the Colonel confided in us and chose us to reveal for the first time in complete detail one of the most astonishing UFO incidents ever reported.

Acknowledgement

The authors express their sincere appreciation to Colonel Robert B. Willingham, a true American hero who gave the best years of his life to defending his country. We thank him for choosing us as the means by which he finally discloses the astonishing story that has haunted him his entire life. When a line was drawn in the sand, he stepped forward to propose that human beings are not the only intelligent species in the universe and that unidentified flying objects really do exist - which makes the Colonel an even greater hero to all of mankind.

Contents

FOREWORD
By Dr. Bruce Maccabee

The book that made the "Roswell Incident" famous was still ten years in the future when a Pennsylvania weekly newspaper published a statement by a Civil Air Patrol pilot about a UFO crash he witnessed in Texas many years earlier. You would think that such a testimony by a pilot would be of great interest to researchers and that they would immediately begin investigating. Unfortunately, skepticism prevailed, and this incredible story was filed away and forgotten for a decade. One of the world's most interesting crash retrieval cases thus lay dormant until an obscure UFO researcher stumbled upon the Pennsylvania newspaper article in 1977 and triggered a series of investigations that eventually led to the publication of this book.

Dr. Bruce Maccabee

The mid to late 1960s was a time of numerous UFO sightings throughout the United States. During this particularly intense period of activity, a most startling case was reported by multiple witnesses in the spring of 1966. Numerous people in the vicinity of Hillsdale and Dexter, Michigan, reported seeing strange lights floating and moving in the sky. In a desperate at-

1

tempt to explain away these disturbing sightings, the Air Force's top civilian UFO consultant, Dr. J. Allen Hynek, suggested that witnesses had seen "swamp gas." After this and other similarly laughable theories were floated by the Air Force, an attitude demanding more information about UFOs arose in America. The U.S. Congress pressured the Air Force to provide funding for a UFO investigation that would be independent of the Air Force's Project Blue Book, which had failed miserably to convince Americans that all UFO sightings had conventional explanations. Thus in 1967, an independent investigation was begun at the University of Colorado, generating a considerable amount of media attention in the UFO subject through the late 1960s and early 1970s.

As a result, it is no surprise that during this period there was a high interest in UFO sightings reported by pilots. The aforementioned article in a Mechanicsburg, Pennsylvania "shopper" newspaper was simply one of many such articles reporting sightings by pilots, law enforcement officers, military officials, and other seemingly reliable and credible observers. But what made this article stand out, in retrospect, is that one of the pilots interviewed in Pennsylvania stated unequivocally that he witnessed the crash of an Alien Flying Craft.

The newspaper article was clipped and mailed to the headquarters of what was then the world's largest civilian group dedicated to the investigation of UFO sightings, the National Investigations Committee on Aerial Phenomena (NICAP). The article was filed along with hundreds of other sighting reports and forgotten. The article languished for ten years before being spotted by Walter Todd Zechel who was reading through the NICAP files looking for interesting sighting reports. This one immediately caught his interest, and he decided to contact the witness. Zechel soon became convinced that this was, indeed, a credible story of a crashed Alien Flying Craft.

The credibility of this story is based on the character and life experiences of one Robert Burton Willingham, a retired colonel in the U.S. Air Force Reserve. While flying a North American F-

FOREWORD

86 Sabre fighter jet during a routine mission in 1955, he, and other pilots in his group, witnessed a bright object streaking through the sky. Willingham saw the object, which had been tracked by radar, make an abrupt "right angle" turn and streak over the horizon near the Texas-Mexico border. Subsequently radar indicated that it had crashed. Willingham obtained permission to leave the mission to try to find the object that had crashed. He found it in the Mexican desert just south of Langtry, Texas. He then returned to his mission. But he was not satisfied with merely flying over the wreckage. He wanted a close up view, so a few hours later he and a co-pilot managed to fly to the crash area in a small plane and land in the desert.

By this time Mexican military had cordoned off the area. The soldiers implied that they were waiting for Americans to come and take it away. The Mexicans ordered Willingham to leave the area, and he did, but not before picking up a piece of strange metal from the object. Several days later he flew over the same area and saw that it was "clean," not a fragment of the device was left in the desert. He reported what he had discovered to the Air Force soon after it happened. He was warned to never talk about it again, and he did not -- for ten years.

If the only evidence were Willingham's sighting of the object this event could, potentially, have been explained away by the Air Force as the crash of an advanced military device. However, this explanation became unlikely when, a few days later, Willingham tested the metal by various means at his disposal. He began to suspect this fragment had been fabricated by technology not known to mankind.

About twelve years later, after being himself involved with UFO investigations for the Air Force (!), Willingham broke his silence and told a reporter from a small Pennsylvania newspaper that he saw a crashed saucer near the Texas-Mexico border in the middle 1950s. However, as pointed out previously, his story was ignored for another ten years.

When Todd Zechel "discovered" Willingham in 1977 and began interviewing him, the investigation into the now-famous

3

"Roswell incident" had not yet begun (it started in late 1978). Up to this time, for most people, the idea that a flying saucer had crashed and had been captured by the U.S. government was considered somewhere between completely unfounded and completely preposterous. This general incredulity resulted from the U.S. military's many years of effective denials, as in the Roswell case, where top Air Force brass immediately held a news conference to announce that the crashed UFO was simply a misidentified weather balloon. Amazingly, this flimsiest of cover stories was sufficient to relegate the Roswell crash to the dustbin of history where it rested until 1978. Meanwhile, the investigation of Willingham's story was already underway three years before the first book about the Roswell incident was published in 1980.

The full development of Willingham's story has taken longer than the Roswell investigation even though there is a highly-credible primary witness (other witnesses have vanished or died). The initial investigation was carried on by Zechel who told very few people about his findings. Zechel realized early in the investigation that there were some "gaps" in Willingham's memories, possibly due to the bullying and intimidation he received at the hands of superior officers, who commanded him to "forget" his strange encounter and never to tell anyone about it. Also, his memory may have been affected by a head injury sustained in the Korean War.

A vexing problem during the early investigation was that initially Willingham did not give the exact year of his UFO encounter. This, combined with other information described in this book, led Zechel and others (including me) to place the event on December 6, 1950, a date when undisputed documentation shows that the U.S. military went on high alert because a group of about forty unidentified "aircraft" were detected approaching the USA from the northeastern area over Canada, along a path that could have been used by long range Russian bombers. These aircraft were never identified and their radar reflections simply "faded out" over US territory. Thus the threat was seemingly gone, but two days later the FBI was told that the Air Intelligence was on "immediate high alert" for any information about flying saucers. For various reasons mentioned in this book, Zechel believed that this alert was caused by the crash witnessed by Willingham. However, information published here for the first time about Willingham's life history makes it clear that the crash took place more than four years after the "high alert." On the other hand, other evidence suggests that there may have been a separate UFO crash in Southwest Texas on December 6, 1950.

The story of Willingham's life is fascinating even without the crashed saucer story. He served in WWII and the Korean War and, for a time in the early 1960s was a UFO sighting investigator for the Air Force! All of his other life experiences provide the background of credibility for what he has to say about the saucer crash. Adding to that credibility is the investigation done by authors Noe Torres and Ruben Uriarte who have presented Willingham's story in a very engaging manner with plenty of supporting information. I believe that the reader will find this book important support for the idea that Alien Flying Craft have crashed on earth and have been retrieved and covered up by the United States Government.

Bruce Maccabee
March 2008

PROLOGUE
The Age of the Super Bomb

"It is part of my responsibility as Commander in Chief of the armed forces to see to it that our country is able to defend itself against any possible aggressor. Accordingly, I have directed the Atomic Energy Commission to continue its work on all forms of atomic weapons, including the so-called hydrogen or super bomb." - *President Harry S. Truman, January 31, 1950.*

In the middle 1950s, at the height of the Cold War, unidentified flying objects were being seen throughout the United States in alarming numbers. To the horror of the U.S. military, UFOs were often seen near high-security military installations, and Air Force pilots and other military personnel frequently reported UFO sightings. Even as the U.S. introduced the first thermonuclear weapons into an already tense world situation, UFOs seemed to serve as omnipresent witnesses to humankind's rapidly deteriorating condition.

"Ivy Mike," the World's First Thermonuclear Bomb Test

This was a period when Cold War tensions brought the entire world to the brink of a nuclear war. In its 1953 assessment of the likelihood of a nuclear war, Chicago's *Bulletin of the Atomic Scientists* set its Doomsday Clock at two minutes before midnight, the closest it has ever been to the end of the world. "Only a few more swings of the pendulum, and, from Moscow to Chicago, atomic explosions will strike midnight for Western civilization," the *Bulletin* observed. "After much debate, the United States decides to pursue the hydrogen bomb, a weapon far more powerful than any atomic bomb. In October 1952, the United States tests its first thermonuclear device, obliterating a Pacific Ocean islet in the process; nine months later, the Soviets test an H-bomb of their own."

In the midst of this troubled time, a remarkable UFO event occurred along the border between Texas and Mexico that has been the source of mystery and speculation for over half a century. It involved an Air Force pilot named Robert Willingham, who one day in the middle 1950s had a UFO encounter that forever changed his life. We call it the "other Roswell," as it relates so closely to the world-famous crash of a UFO near Roswell, New Mexico, in 1947.

Willingham's story of having visited the site of a UFO crash along the Texas-Mexico border first surfaced in 1967 and has been mentioned in a number of books and publications since then. It was known to a few UFO researchers long before Jesse Marcel, Sr. came forward in 1978 with the remarkable tale of his involvement in the famous UFO crash near Roswell, New Mexico in 1947, which subsequently spawned the "Roswell phenomenon."

This book, for the first time, tells Robert Willingham's remarkable story of the "other Roswell" in the full detail that only years of thought and reflection can finally bring forward. Willingham has spent most of the years since 1955 wishing that this incident had never happened to him, as it has brought him nothing but pain and misfortune. Nonetheless, he has reached a point where he feels that it is time for this important story to finally be told in its entirety.

"They told me never to say anything or there would be consequences," he says, looking warily out the front window of his modest home near Wichita Falls, Texas. "But I'm 82 years old now, and my health is not too good. There's really not much they can do to me now."

Colonel Willingham At Home, March 2008

1

BEGINNINGS

Life had a simple beginning for the U.S. Air Force pilot who became a legend for stepping out from behind the thick veil of military secrecy to boldly proclaim that, while piloting a jet aircraft, he not only witnessed a UFO streaking across the skies of Texas at 2,000 miles per hour, but he also saw it plunge to earth along the Texas-Mexico border and even visited the crash site, where he picked up a piece of the debris from the still-smoldering wreckage. Born on August 15, 1926 in the tiny Texas town of Holliday, fifteen miles southeast of Wichita Falls, Robert Burton Willingham was, at an early age, known for a keen intellect, strong leadership skills, and a good-natured "country boy" sense of humor, all of which carried forward in his life even to the age of 82, as of the writing of this book.

Ingrained in his personality are a playful feistiness and an inherent resistance to doing something simply because one is ordered to do it. Due to this latter trait, the rebel within him resisted instructions from his military superiors to "shut up" about the UFO incident and warnings that he would suffer "consequences" if he spoke up about it. While so many other military men and women since the 1930s have chosen not to talk about similar events, Willingham defied the norm and saw no harm in letting people know about the unusual incident that he experienced during his flying days.

In many ways, Willingham's personality is as tough as the boom-or-bust area of Texas where he grew up. An economically downtrodden, off-the-beaten path whistle stop early in its history, Holliday, Texas, experienced the mixed blessing of explosive growth in the early 1920s, following the discovery of vast oil deposits all around the town. With the establishment in 1916 of the Panther Oilfield, four miles outside of town, oil

9

wells soon began appearing throughout the area, and Holliday's population surged from 219 in 1925 to 1,000 in 1926.

Robert B. Willingham, Circa 1945

The *Handbook of Texas Online* states, "By 1926 Holliday had one of the county's three independent school districts and a high school. The 1926 *Texas Almanac* describes the town as a large oilfield-supply manufacturing and distribution center with about sixty businesses, including refineries. By then, over 1,400 wells had been drilled in the vicinity, including the largest in the county, the Wilmut well, on the Geraldine town site five miles south of Holliday."

Among the many local people who toiled in the blossoming oilfields of 1926 Holliday was a 31-year-old oil pipeline worker named John R. Willingham, a pipe layer. In August 1926, in the midst of Holliday's newfound economic growth, John and his 22-year-old wife, Bessie, gave birth to Robert Burton Willing-ham, destined to transcend the hardships of life in the Texas oilfields, serve honorably in World War II, receive a purple heart in the Korean War, become a pioneer Air Force jet aviator, and rise up the ranks of the military to become a colonel in the reserves. More importantly, Robert would become one of the few military pilots to go public with an admission that he chased a UFO and that he stood in the midst of a debris field created by the subsequent crash of the object.

Typical Oil Field Work of the Period (Library of Congress)

Attending the schools of Holliday and nearby Archer City in the thirties and forties, Robert proved himself a fast learner whose knowledge and common sense sometimes outpaced those of his teachers. In 1934, at the age of eight, he first learned about the mysterious objects in the sky that people later called "flying saucers." He recalls, "We didn't know back then exactly what to call them. I heard from a boy down the street that his grandfather had seen one. So, we all went down there to his house and heard the story." Little did the youngster realize how much of an impact one of these objects would have on his life in the future.

At age nine, Willingham had another experience that would significantly impact his life. He began hanging around with local aviator, airplane mechanic, and all-around flying enthusiast, Pete Minich. As it turned out, Minich owned a French-built biplane of World War I vintage, and he was only too happy to give the young Willingham free flying lessons. Thus, Robert's fascination with flying and airplanes began at this very early age, and, more importantly, he started logging flight hours.

Pete Minich (center) Taught Willingham How to Fly

In 1938, Willingham and his family moved to Archer City, just a few miles south of Holliday. By the time he reached high school, Willingham had cemented a rugged individualism that blended his father's oilfield work ethic with his own book learning, and he began to have conflicts with the principal of Archer City High School, Mr. Gerring, who made it his mission to set the young man on the straight and narrow. When Willingham resisted, the inevitable tension ensued. Willingham's troubles in school finally came to a head on April 7, 1944, just a few weeks shy of graduation.

"Me and the principal had a little fuss. I got mad and nearly whipped him. Then I quickly walked over to the courthouse and signed up for the Army. Boy, was my mom mad," Willingham remembers. "I always was a little high tempered. I guess it was a little of my Indian blood coming out."

Later, when military officials requested his high school transcripts, he hesitated about contacting Mr. Gerring. As it turned out, his fears were unfounded. The principal went out of his way to personally collect the records that Willingham needed and made sure that they were delivered to the authorities at Camp Hood, Texas, as requested. Willingham so appreciated the gesture that years later, when he returned from overseas service in World War II, he went to personally thank Gerring.

World War I Era French Biplane (Courtesy of Wikipedia.org)

2

THE WORLD AT WAR

When Willingham joined the Army in 1944, the United States was mired in the midst of the Second World War, fighting Nazis in Europe and Japanese in the Pacific. Although the tide was finally starting to turn in the Allies' favor, the Germans were being kicked out of Russia, and D-Day occurred in June, the war had nonetheless already taken a heavy toll on America.

Willingham (inset) Arrives in LaHavre, France

By April 1944, more than 300,000 Americans had already lost their lives in the war, and more than 100,000 would die before hostilities ended in 1945. A total of more than 16 million Americans would serve in the military between 1941 and 1945. To the 17-year-old Willingham, the cause seemed just, the time seemed right, and in 1944, he traded his high school textbooks for the battlefield gear of the U.S. Army.

Pontoon Bridge across the Rhine River in 1945 (U.S. Army Photo)

Arriving at Camp Hood, Texas, Willingham underwent an accelerated basic training necessitated by the war. He let it be known that he desired to be a pilot. When an officer pointed out, "But you only have a high school education," Willingham replied, "What's that got to do with flying?" He explained that he had been flying since the age of nine, which probably impressed the listeners and resulted in a note being placed in his personnel file. Nonetheless, the decision was made that he should start off his military career as a combat engineer.He was quickly shipped off to serve with General George S. Patton's 288th Combat Engineers under the umbrella of the Army's 82nd Airborne Division. His first deployment was to the northern French sea port town of Le Havre, which was liberated as a result of the U.S and Allied invasion of Normandy in June 1944. Willingham worked for several weeks to clear all the sunken boats out of the local waterways, thus enabling ships with troops and equipment to move through safely. Suddenly, the young man who only weeks before had been striding down the halls of his high school in Archer City was helping prepare the way for some of the war's most important battles.

Officially a "bridge company," Willingham's group spent much of its time working on bridges in support of troop movements. The company's duties included checking bridges prior to troop crossings, inspecting and shoring up damaged bridges, building footbridges for infantry, and also constructing pontoon bridges to allow for the crossing of waterways. As part of his role, Willingham helped inspect the bridges that were used by General Patton prior to leading his troops across the Rhine River into Germany.

Willingham in Garmisch, Germany. Circa 1946.

The bright and industrious young Texan caught the eye of Army leadership, and he rapidly climbed to the rank of lieutenant. Also during this period, he landed the important task of finding temporary housing for General Patton, who needed a place to set up battlefield operations. Willingham found an abandoned castle and coordinated a rapid clean-up and maintenance operation using German prisoners of war. Patton subsequently found the arrangement quite to his liking. "That old man had the best battle tactics of anyone we had in our army," Willingham remembers of Patton. "He just was a little bit hot tempered, that's all."

In one of his most memorable missions of this period, Willingham was part of a task force given the responsibility of traveling into Russia to retrieve 24 U.S. Army trucks that had been leased to the Soviet Union. When Willingham and his team arrived in Russia, they discovered that, due to a misunderstanding, the Soviets had no intention of giving up the trucks. During the night, Willingham and the other Americans sneaked into the trucks and quickly drove them away. The Russians gave chase for while, before finally giving up.For two years following the defeat of the Nazis in 1945, Willingham served as a Provost Marshal in the Allied occupational force in Munich. His tasks included delivering bread, coal, and other supplies needed by the war-ravaged city of Munich.

Upon his return to the U.S., Willingham remained in the Army and later drew an assignment to assist with operations for an Air Force airlift squadron. Evidently, someone in the Air Force brass took notice of his hours of flying a French biplane with Pete Minich back in Texas, because a commanding officer took him aside one day in 1950 and announced, "You are now a member of the United States Air Force, son."

Willingham looked at the officer incredulously and replied, almost involuntarily, "Oh no, I'm not. I'm Army."

"You have been officially reassigned to serve in the Air Force," the officer said. "Congratulations."

3

KOREAN NIGHTMARE

As it turned out, with the Korean War gaining momentum, the Air Force needed pilots, and Robert Willingham was tabbed to help fill the urgent need. After undergoing accelerated pilot training, Willingham arrived in Korea in the fall of 1950 and began flying missions in support of ground troops. His main role was to use his P-51 Mustang to dive and lay down strafing fire in advance of U.S. troop movements. The P-51 was a long-range, single-seat fighter, for which Willingham to this day expresses a great admiration.

P-51 Mustang Similar to Willingham's (USAF Museum Archives)

KOREAN NIGHTMARE

On December 27, 1950, after only four months in Korea, Willingham had the grave misfortune of being wounded on the ground when his position came under enemy fire. As bullets rained down around him, he remembers being handed an M-1 rifle by a Marine who was running around dispensing weapons and telling everyone to take cover and fight back. Scrambling for the safety of a foxhole, Willingham was suddenly rocked by a mortar shell that sent him flying through the air, embedding shrapnel in his legs. "I got blown out a hole. I almost lost both legs, and they got 52 pieces of shrapnel out of me," he remembers.

He was flown out for medical treatment, first to Tokyo General Hospital and then on to an Air Force hospital in San Antonio, Texas, where he arrived early in 1951. "They worked on me in San Antonio and were able to save my legs," he says, "They operated on my left knee two more times after that and fixed it up real good."

Although his legs were soon healed and virtually back to normal, Willingham sustained a much more serious injury that doctors did not catch and that would not fully surface until many years in the future. When the mortar shell exploded near him and sent him hurtling headlong, he suffered a head injury that eventually resulted in a restriction of the flow of blood to his brain. This caused him further health problems in the mid sixties. "I got hit in the head, and when the scar tissue formed, it closed up one of the veins coming into my brain."

Nonetheless, with the effects of the head injury still many years in the future, Willingham set about the business of getting his leg injuries healed up in order to resume flying. Told by military doctors that he could no longer fly combat missions, Willingham opted to continue his flying career in the Air Force Reserve. By doing so, he enjoyed a lot more flying time than he would have gotten if he had remained in the regular Air Force.

Willingham remembers being "out of action" for most of 1951 and then slowly working his way back into flying shape. In his new role as a reservist, he resumed his status as a pilot in

1952, flying mainly North American P-51 Mustangs, B-25s, AT-6s, P-40s, and P-47s. As the military continued transitioning to jets, Willingham put in flight time on the Lockheed T-33 Shooting Star jet trainer, F-86 Sabres, and F-84 Thunderjets.

Willingham's F-84a Thunderjet, Circa 1952

Willingham continued flying on numerous training and aircraft testing missions for the rest of the 1950s, as part of the Cold War effort to remain at constant readiness for the possibility of a nuclear war against the Soviet Union. It was during one of his stateside flying missions after his return from Korea that Willingham had an experience that, whether he liked it or not, would define and shape the rest of his life. On a sunny, warm day in the Southwest, Willingham flew an F-86 Sabre jet from Carlswell Air Force Base in Fort Worth, Texas, on a training run to provide "cover" for a B-47 bomber headed first to El Paso and then north to Washington state, when suddenly, a chance encounter with a fast-moving UFO forever altered things. Looking back now, at the age of 82, he often finds himself wishing that it had never taken place.

In the wake of bullying and intimidation by his military superiors to keep quiet about what he saw, Willingham survived another decade of military service by temporarily putting the UFO incident out of his mind and focusing on the tasks at hand. It was by doing so that his career moved forward, and he was able to progress up the ranks to become a colonel in the Air Force Reserve. Had he gone public with his story in the late fifties or early sixties, Willingham is convinced that he would have immediately faced the dire "consequences" with which he was threatened. The level of intimidation to which he was subjected caused him to avoid talking about what happened or writing anything down on paper even for his own future recollection.

Willingham Points to His Name at the Archer County Veterans Memorial, March 2008

As a result of this voluntary memory suppression, when Willingham finally did come forward with his story in 1967, he did not recall the exact date of his UFO encounter. Still, although the date may be fuzzy, he remains firmly convinced of what he witnessed and of the incredible experience he went through following his encounter.

BRIGHT STAR

During the mid fifties, Willingham, who now held the rank of major, participated in many Cold War air simulations over the skies of the Western United States. Among the early military objectives of this period was the breaking in of two of history's most awesome bomber aircraft, Boeing's B-47 and B-52.

Jet-Assisted B-47 Takeoff, Trailed by F-80 (USAF Photo)

As the world's first swept-wing jet bomber aircraft, the B-47 was an awesome achievement in military aviation, and it gave the U.S. an important advantage in its Cold War standoff with the Soviet Union. The huge bomber was designed to incorporate some of the features of a jet fighter, such as swept wings, a bubble canopy, and engine modifications. The B-47 typically carried three crewmembers, including a pilot, copilot, and a combination navigator, bombardier, and radar operator. Should war break out between the U.S. and U.S.S.R., the B-47s were the aircraft that would penetrate Soviet air defenses and deliver America's nuclear response onto key Russian targets in the early to mid fifties.

On one particular day in 1955, Major Robert Willingham drew the assignment of participating in the escort of several bombers coming into Texas from New York and headed first to El Paso and then on to Washington state. Willingham recalls that the bombers were mostly B-47s but the group may also have included some B-52s, which were starting to work their way into service. Each bomber was to be escorted by four jet fighters, as the big aircraft moved over the Lone Star State. Once they reached El Paso, the bombers would head up one of the flight paths designated by the U.S. Strategic Air Command for reaching the Soviet Union in the event of a nuclear confrontation, via the West Coast, Canada, and Alaska.

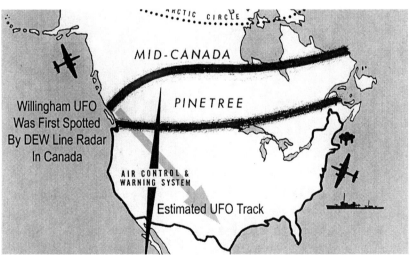

Diagram of the DEW System. The Pinetree and Mid-Canada Lines Were Operational in 1952. (USAF Photo)

Along with three other F-86 aviators assigned to shadow one of the B-47s, Willingham departed Carswell Air Force Base on what, at the time, appeared to be just another routine training mission. His aircraft carried serial number CD-195, and his call sign was "Willie Eddie." Willingham's group headed out of Fort Worth toward El Paso, passing near Abilene and then San Angelo. It was early afternoon on a bright early spring day.

Willingham remembers that the squadron had received intelligence by radio that a fast-moving unidentified aircraft had been picked up by the Distant Early Warning (DEW) radar system, located in Canada. The UFO was moving south toward Texas.

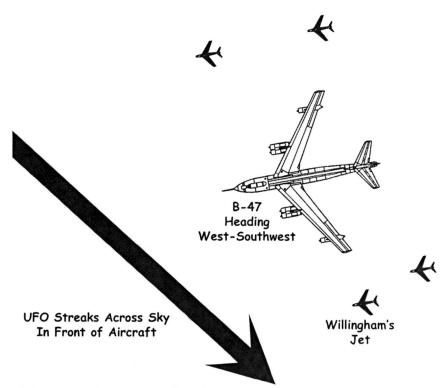

Illustration Based on Willingham's Sketch of the Flight Formation

The next mention of an unidentified flying object came from the pilot of the B-47 he was escorting, whose voice crackled on Willingham's cockpit radio about an unknown aircraft he had picked up on radar moving toward them from a generally northwest heading. Willingham states, "One of the bomber pilots called me and asked what it was that I saw about twenty degrees ahead of us. By his radar, he could tell it was coming our way. I looked up and saw a big, bright object that looked like a star, but I knew it couldn't be a star."

Intensely luminous even in the daylight sky, the UFO streaked past the squadron at a speed that Willingham later estimated at over 2,000 miles per hour. The object passed within 35 to 40 miles of the squadron, headed generally east-southeast. "It was just a big, bright light," he remembers. All four fighter pilots who were escorting the B-47 observed the UFO as it zoomed past, headed south toward the Texas-Mexico border.

An F-86 Sabre like Willingham's Jet (USAF Photo)

Willingham's description of the UFO sounds almost exactly like that of a luminous flying disc seen during a 1957 case involving a B-47 that was flying over the skies of the South Central U.S. The 1957 case was first brought to light in 1967 by the pilot and two crewmembers that experienced it. Included as case number five in Edward U. Condon's 1969 book *Final Report of the Scientific Study of Unidentified Flying Objects* (commonly called *The Condon Report*), it is an astounding tale of a harrowing UFO encounter that occurred within a year or two after Willingham's case.On the 19th or 20th of September, 1957, a large, intensely bright fireball – alternating in color from white to red – chased an Air Force RB-47 for more than 600 miles over a period of more than an hour. During the chase, the mysterious object was seen visually by the plane's crew, was detected by ground radar at Carswell Air Force Base in Fort Worth, and was also picked up by direction-finding radar installed on the RB-47. Dr. James E. McDonald, a University of Arizona professor who investigated the case, was impressed that "three independent sensing systems ... were giving seemingly consistent indications: two pairs of human eyes, a ground radar, and a direction-finding radar receiver in the aircraft."

Adding to the credibility of the case is that fact that the RB-47's special equipment for electronic reconnaissance and electronic countermeasures (ECM) registered a strong radar signal emanating from the unidentified flying object at a frequency of 2,800 megacycles. Also, the UFO exhibited performance characteristics that ruled out the possibility it was any kind of conventional or secret military aircraft, just as in the Willingham encounter.

Shortly after the strange radar contact was first picked up, pilot Lewis D. Chase of Spokane, Washington, spotted what he first thought were the landing lights of another jet approaching from his eleven o'clock position. Chase then realized the oncoming object was a single, very bright white light, closing fast. The *Condon* report stated, "Before any evasive action could be taken, the light crossed in front of the plane, moving to the right, at a velocity far higher than airplane speeds. The light was seen by pilot and co-pilot, and appeared to the pilot to be a glowing body as big as a barn."

RB-47e Stratojet, Circa 1960 (USAF Photo)

After rapidly moving to the two o'clock position, the intense white light then "winked" out. Although no longer visible, the strange object's signature was still being detected by the ECM gear aboard the RB-47. The UFO was keeping pace with their aircraft.

After about a hundred miles of flight, the RB-47 came within the radar-coverage area of Carswell Air Force Base Ground Controlled Intercept (GCI) station. Chase, the pilot, contacted Carswell to ask if they detected any other air traffic near their position. Carlswell immediately radioed back that there was another "aircraft" within ten miles of them at their two o'clock position. Whereas the RB-47 was identifiable on radar by its transponder signal, the other object had no such signal and appeared only as a radar blip.

Sketch of GCI Radar Station (U.S. Navy Photo)

As Carswell radar continued to track both aircraft, the UFO next moved to the twelve o'clock position dead ahead of the plane, holding a ten-mile range, and again became visible to the eye as a huge, steady, red glow. Chase described the object as "bigger than a house." The pilot went to maximum speed. The target appeared to stop, and as the plane got close to it and flew over it, the target simply "winked out." Not only did it disappear from view, but it also vanished from both the plane's direction-finding radar and the ground based radar.

Moments later, as the plane flew over Mineral Wells, Texas, the object reappeared as a bright red light. "The pilot received permission from Ground Control to change altitude, and dove the plane at the target, which appeared stationary. As the plane approached to an estimated distance of five miles, the target vanished again from both visual observation and radar."

In a chilling footnote, the *Condon* report states, "According to the officer, upon return to the [Air Force base] electronic counter-measures, graphic data, and radar scope pictures which had been taken during the flight were removed from the plane by Intelligence personnel." The plane was met immediately on the ground by an intelligence officer assigned to the base, who quickly took all filmed and wire-recorded data from the crew at the radar monitoring area on the back end of the plane. Also, crewmembers were later debriefed, and some were extensively interrogated.

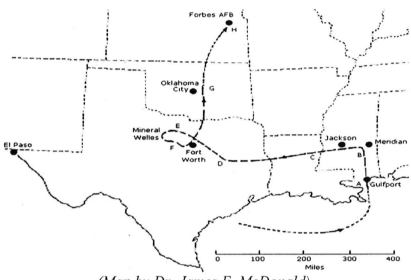

(Map by Dr. James E. McDonald)

Regardless of whether or not this case is directly linked to Willingham's story, it certainly provides insight into possible reasons why the incident involving Willingham was never revealed by the military, why he was pressured to not speak about it, and why none of the other aviators involved seem to have spoken out either. As revealed in the *Condon* B-47 case, a tight lid of secrecy was immediately slammed shut, evidence was made to "disappear," and the airmen involved were carefully "debriefed" by intelligence operatives.

In a related development, the Central Intelligence Agency recently declassified a memorandum about a UFO event that occurred on September 20, 1957. It is one of the first declassified CIA documents to mention UFOs and relates an event that may have a connection to the *Condon* RB-47 case and possibly even the Willingham case.

BRIGHT STAR

21 September 1957

MEMORANDUM FOR: Acting Director, Central Intelligence

SUBJECT   : Unidentified Flying Object Reported on 20 September 1957

1. As reported by components of the US Air Defense Command, an unidentified flying object (UFO) was tracked by US radars on a relatively straight course from the eastern tip of Long Island to the vicinity of Buffalo. The object was reportedly moving westward at an altitude of 50,000 feet and speed of 2,000 kts. "Jamming" was reported by several radars in this vicinity and westward as far as Chicago. In a subsequent briefing for representatives of the IAC, the US Air Force reported that the original reports had been degraded somewhat by information that: (a) there was an 11 minute break in the track; (b) weather conditions in the area were of the type which have in the past produced false radar pips and electronic interference; (c) B-47's of SAC were in the area near Chicago on an ECM training flight. The ADC has not completed its investigation of this incident, but in any event it now seems clear that the phenomena reported west of Buffalo were not related to the UFO.

The UFO Memo from 9-20-57 (CIA FOIA Web Site)

The CIA memo states, "As reported by components of the US Air Defense Command, an unidentified flying object (UFO) was tracked by US radars on a relatively straight course from the eastern tip of Long Island to the vicinity of Buffalo. The object was reportedly moving westward at an altitude of 50,000 feet and speed of 2,000 knots. 'Jamming' was reported by several radars in this vicinity and westward as far as Chicago. In a subsequent briefing for representatives of the IAC, the US Air Force reported that the original reports had been degraded somewhat by information that: (a) there was an 11 minute break in the tracks; (b) weather conditions in the area were of the type which have in the past produced false radar pips and electronic interference; (c) B-47s of SAC were in the area near Chicago on an ECM training flight."

The memo, which mentions other RB-47s equipped with ECM equipment, makes clear that, far from ignoring UFOs (as the CIA has long claimed it does), the agency took an active interest in the topic, at least in the mid to late fifties. According to the memo, this UFO incident was so significant that a briefing was held "for representatives of the IAC [Intelligence Advisory Committee]."

If Robert Willingham had been just another military pilot who witnessed a UFO whizzing past him, the U.S. intelligence community would probably have shown little interest. But, something incredible was about to happen in Willingham's case. The glowing fireball that he saw streaking past him in the skies over central Texas was about to crash-land, and soon Willingham would stand in the very debris field where it slammed into the earth.

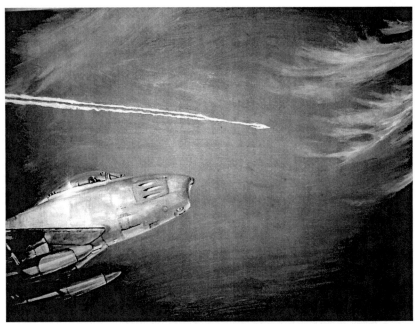

Painting of UFO Streaking Past an F-86 by Patrick Richards of Socorro, New Mexico (Used by Permission)

5

TURNABOUT INTRUDER

Robert Willingham received a call from the pilot of the B-47 that he was escorting, and the alarmed voice informed him that a UFO was closing in fast on their position from a generally west heading. Looking in the direction indicated, Willingham observed a fast-moving bright streak of light traveling at an altitude of about 50,000 feet and watched it approach within 35 or 40 miles of his jet aircraft. He estimated the object's speed at three or four times that of his own aircraft, which was capable of 685 miles per hour. He later described the brightly lit surface of the object as looking "like magnesium steel."

The startled aviator then witnessed something that completely shocked him. Willingham recalls, "At about that time, it made a 90-degree turn to the right doing about 2,000 miles an hour, and I knew it wasn't an airplane. We didn't have anything that could do that. We don't have anything that can do that even now."

After executing the 90-degree turn, the UFO headed south toward the Mexico border in the general direction (but slightly west) of Del Rio, Texas. Willingham remembers, "We got to watching how it made a 90 degree turn at this high speed and everything. We knew it wasn't a missile of any type."

Shortly after the object turned to the south, Willingham noticed that "there were a lot of sparks, and it tilted down by about a 45-degree angle." He remembers thinking at the time that the UFO's abrupt turning maneuver possibly caused damage to the integrity of the airship's hull.

As he listened to the chatter on the radio and continued making his own visual observations, Willingham noted that the UFO continued streaking southward across Texas toward a point near the border city of Del Rio, located on the Rio Grande River. The object continued listing and descending at about a 45-degree angle. Perhaps the saucer's occupants were having trouble controlling their craft. As the steady descent continued, the object fell out of Willingham's view, and he assumed it had crash-landed somewhere just west of Del Rio.

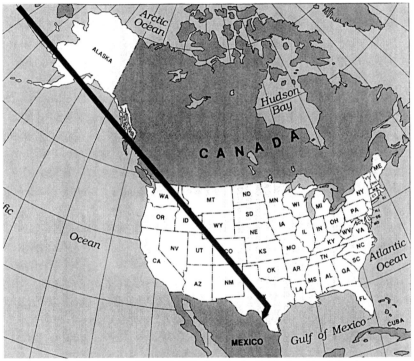

Estimated UFO Flight Path (UT-Austin Map)

He later concluded that when the UFO approached the Texas-Mexico border, it dropped out of the sky and slammed into the desert floor just beyond the southern edge of the Rio Grande River, about 50 miles west-northwest of Del Rio. The burning hot object skidded on the sandy soil for several hundred feet before coming to rest against a sandy mound, where it continued to generate intense heat for hours afterward.

Radar observers tracked the object until it went off their screens and became convinced that the object had crashed and was now on the ground somewhere near Del Rio. According to Willingham, the radar controllers "kept following it, and they claimed that it crashed somewhere off between Texas and the Mexico border."

The other aviators who were in Willingham's escort group on that day also witnessed the same luminous orb streaking across the sky. Two of his fellow F-86 pilots later admitted to their base commander, during a debriefing that Willingham also attended, that they had seen the mysterious object. Willingham, however, was the only one of the group who was willing to speak up about it.

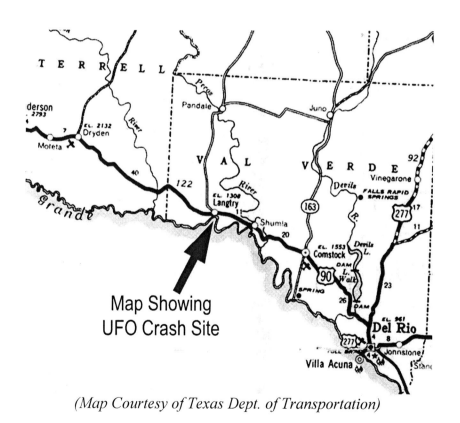

Map Showing
UFO Crash Site

(Map Courtesy of Texas Dept. of Transportation)

Based on his own observations and the subsequent talk on the military radio, Willingham estimated that the UFO had crash-landed very close to a famous historical landmark in Texas, Judge Roy Bean's Saloon and Courthouse, located in Langtry. Willingham knew the place very well, because, as he recalls, "I used to hunt deer there." Eager to go look at the fallen object, he radioed the flight commander to ask permission to make a quick flight down to the crash site. "I called the guy that was flying the B-47 and told him I'd like to go look at it. He said to hold on."

"He then called Denver, which controlled all of our flights at that time, and he called me back and said, 'Yes, go check what it was and where it hit. We want to know what it was, too.' So, I took off."

The B-47 pilot also instructed Willingham to file a complete report about what he saw upon his return to base. Willingham assured him that he would do so just as soon as he returned to Carswell.

Breaking off from the formation, Willingham made the quick flight from near San Angelo down to Langtry, a distance of about 150 air miles. Bringing his F-86 down to the unsafe altitude of 800 feet, he saw the still-smoldering wreckage of a disc-shaped object on the ground, just south of the Rio Grande River, directly across from Langtry. "I flew over there and looked it over. I got down to about 800 feet, which you're not allowed to do, you know. I got down there where I could see what I wanted to see and then went on back to pick up my B-47 once again."

Although obligated to continue with his mission, Willingham began formulating a plan in his mind to come back to the crash site after returning his jet aircraft to base. He was determined to find out more about the mysterious object that streaked across Texas and was now lodged in the earth just across the Rio Grande River from Langtry.

He was supposed to remain alongside the bombers until they reached El Paso, at which point another group of jets would take over the escort duties. However, He noticed that his fuel was running low. "By that time I was just about dried up, and I told them that I had to get back to base." Willingham requested and received permission to head back to Carswell Air Force Base in Fort Worth.

As he pointed his fighter jet back to home base, Willingham tried to make sense of the day's strange events. What was the object he had seen? How could it perform maneuvers that no jet or missile could execute? What caused it to go down?

As he thought about the UFO's crash, it was clear that nobody from his squadron had fired at the object. Could other jets have fired on it earlier? Could it have been struck by a surface-to-air missile?

In the book *The Report on Unidentified Flying Objects*, author Edward J. Ruppelt, the former head of *Project Blue Book*, mentions a 1952 case in which an F-86 Sabre, just like Willingham's, fired on a UFO. Ruppelt was summoned to an unnamed U.S. fighter base, where the base intelligence officer took him to a private room, unlocked a safe, and produced a thick report. The officer told Ruppelt it was the only remaining copy, as all other documentation about the case had been ordered destroyed.

The report revealed that at 10 a.m. a few weeks prior, base radar had picked up an unidentified object closing fast from the northeast at about 700 miles per hour. Two F-86s were scrambled to pursue the bogey, but radar had trouble maintaining a fix on it, as it seemed to fade in and out of the scopes.

After a period of searching, one of the F-86s spotted the UFO at an altitude of 3,000 feet, cruising along at over 700 miles per hour. Ruppelt wrote, "... the pilot pushed the nose of the F-86 down and started after the object. He closed fairly fast, until he came to within an estimated 1,000 yards. Now he could get a good look at the object. Although it had looked like a balloon from above, a closer view showed that it was definitely round and flat saucer shaped. The pilot described it as being 'like a doughnut without a hole.'"

The F-86 pilot, who had lost communication with base, closed to within 500 feet, but the UFO suddenly began to speed away. Unable to receive instructions from base, the pilot decided to fire. Ruppelt wrote, "It was like a David about to do battle with a Goliath, but he had to take a chance. Quickly charging his guns, he started shooting.... A moment later the object pulled up into a climb and in a few seconds it was gone. The pilot climbed to 10,000 feet, called the other F-86, and now was able to contact his buddy. They joined up and went back to their base."

After letting Ruppelt read the report and take notes, the base intelligence officer burned it, as he had previously been instructed to do. Ruppelt observed, "The commanding officer of the fighter group, a full colonel and command pilot, believed that UFOs were real. The colonel believed in UFOs because he had a lot of faith in his pilots -- and they had chased UFO's in their F-86s. He had seen UFOs on the scopes of his radar sets, and he knew radar."

Robert Willingham had heard about some of these other UFO encounters by fighter jets, but he refused to believe that it could ever happen to him. However, on the day he saw a ball of light streak across the Texas sky and crash near Langtry, the UFO enigma suddenly became very real to him.

6

JUDGE ROY BEAN'S PLACE

For Robert Willingham, the location of the UFO crash site was no mystery, as he had visited the area on several occasions while on deer hunting expeditions. Also, a few months before the UFO encounter, he had assisted the U.S. Border Patrol with surveillance operations by flying a Piper Super Cruiser along the Rio Grande River in the Del Rio sector. Willingham was well familiar with the unique history of this fascinating area of the Lone Star State, including the outrageous antics of the region's best-known historical figure, Judge Roy Bean.

1900 Photo (Courtesy of the U.S. National Archives)

From the time he first spoke up about his UFO encounter, Willingham stated that the unknown object crashed "just across the river from Judge Roy Bean's place." This location refers to the combination saloon and courtroom of one of the Old West's most colorful characters, which still stands in Langtry and is now a tourist attraction maintained by the Texas Department of Transportation.

Sometime around 1882, saloonkeeper Roy Bean, a native of Kentucky, set up shop in a small tent city on a bluff overlooking the Rio Grande River. That odd assortment of tents eventually grew into the town of Langtry. Due to recurring problems with outlaws from both Mexico and the U.S., the state's law enforcement officials were looking for any help they could get along the border, and they appointed Bean as a county justice of the peace, although Bean himself had reportedly once fled a murder charge in New Mexico and was known to occasionally dabble in smuggling. With very little formal education and virtually no knowledge of the law, Bean proceeded to dispense justice by relying on common sense and his own whims.

View South Toward the Rio Grande River at Langtry

Among the stories (or legends) told about him is a case where a Chinese railroad worker was shot dead in Langtry one day. Leafing quickly through the one law book he possessed, Bean ruled that he could find no law against killing a "Chinaman," and he dismissed the case. On another occasion, a man, who had been shot to death, was found to have on his person forty dollars in cash and a pistol. Bean fined the corpse forty dollars for carrying a concealed weapon and used the money for burial expenses.

Bean, who was also known for keeping a beer-drinking bear chained up behind his saloon, in 1896, arranged an historic world heavyweight championship-boxing match between Bob Fitzsimmons and Bob Maher. Due to opposition from religious groups seeking to curtail gambling, authorities in both the U.S. and Mexico had banned the fight. Bean stepped in and offered to hold the bout on a small "spit" of land on the Mexican side of the Rio Grande River across from Langtry. The *Texas Handbook Online* states, "[Roy Bean] reached his peak of notoriety with his staging of the match between Peter Maher of Ireland and Bob Fitzsimmons of Australia. The fight was opposed by civic and religious leaders such as Baptist missionary Leander Millican, and both the Mexican and the U.S. governments had prohibited it. Bean arranged to hold it on the Mexican side of the Rio Grande, knowing the Mexican authorities could not conveniently reach the site, and that Woodford H. Mabry's Texas Rangers would have no jurisdiction. The spectators arrived aboard a chartered train; after a profitable delay contrived by Bean, the crowd witnessed Fitzsimmons's defeat of Maher in less than two minutes."

Ironically, it was not far from where Fitzsimmons and Maher fought in 1896 that Willingham saw the remains of a flying saucer that had slammed into the sandy soil on the Mexican side, skidded about 300 yards, and then had come to a stop against two sand mounds. According to Willingham, the fallen object could easily be observed from the U.S. side of the river.

In fact, later on the day of the crash, Willingham spoke with a Langtry resident who lived very close to the river and witnessed the entire incident. Willingham asked the man if he saw the object crash land, and he replied "I sure did, and it scared the hell out of me! I was working in the backyard, and all of a sudden I saw a fireball come across the sky. It like to scared me to death!"

Arrow Shows UFO Trajectory Shortly Before Crashing
(Texas Dept. of Transportation)

Willingham gazed to where the man's house stood, not too far from the river, and replied, "I don't blame you for being scared. If that thing had come in about ten feet lower, it probably would have taken the roof of your house."

In the above map, Roy Bean's saloon is marked with a star. It is located on Spur 25, which branches off from U.S. Highway 90 leading east to Del Rio and west to Sanderson. The tiny community of Langtry, now consisting largely of crumbling ruins, extends southward to the northern bank of the Rio Grande River. It is just south of there, several hundred feet into Mexican territory, that the fireball struck, spewing metallic debris as it gouged a long furrow in the earth.

Historical Marker near UFO Crash Site (2007 by Noe Torres)

FLIGHT OF DISCOVERY

Even as Robert Willingham saw the UFO streak down toward the Mexican border and disappear, a strong desire to find out more surged within him. "I saw more or less where it hit while I was flying," he recalls. "I told the flight commander that I was going to fly over it [the crash site] and come back." The commander replied, "Okay, we want to know what it is."

Willingham (middle) with Fellow Pilots, Early 60s

After making the quick jaunt down to Langtry in his F-86, he determined that the crash site was right across the Rio Grande River from Judge Roy Bean's place. Risking a low-altitude fly-over, he spotted the still-smoldering wreckage of the disc-shaped object on the south side of the Rio Grande River, a few hundred feet into Mexican territory. "I got down there where I could see what I wanted to see and then went on back to pick up my B-47 once again."

Although obligated to resume his mission, Willingham was determined to return to the scene of the crash in a smaller aircraft that could be set down on the ground in the relatively tight spaces afforded by rocky ledges south of Langtry. After his fuel registered low, Willingham was allowed to fly back to base, where he quickly turned in his jet and stowed his gear.

Willingham asked a fellow fighter pilot, Lieutenant Colonel James P. Morgan of Fort Worth, if Morgan would give him a lift down to the Corsicana Air Field, located about 50 miles away, where Willingham intended to pick up a small plane and fly to the scene of the UFO crash. Morgan, who had participated in the mission earlier that day, agreed to take Willingham to Corsicana. The two men flew out of Carswell Air Force Base in Morgan's private plane, a Piper Cub. They arrived a few minutes later in Corsicana, where Willingham's Civil Air Patrol unit was based.

Corsicana was the site of the World War II era Corsicana Air Field, and the Air Force Reserve used one of the hangers there for storing some of its aircraft. Willingham remembers the base fondly, "Ah, it had the best runway they had in the country. It ran north south, and the prevailing winds ran north all the time there. Boy, it was a good place to fly out of."

After arriving in Corsicana, Willingham ran into a buddy named Jack Perkins, an electrical engineer from Pennsylvania who served in Willingham's Civil Air Patrol unit. Perkins worked on airplane navigation systems and other electrical components of aircraft. On this particular afternoon, Willingham found Perkins in one of the hangers at the Corsicana Air Field, working on the electrical systems of one of the planes housed there. "He was a *helluva* electronic engineer," Willingham recalls. "He was first class."

Realizing he needed someone to corroborate his story, Willingham told Perkins about the UFO encounter and asked if he would accompany Willingham down to the border to look at the crashed object. Perkins immediately expressed a strong interest in going. "He definitely wanted to go down there to look where it hit," Willingham remembers.

The two men got out a two-passenger light plane called an Aeronca Champion, which was used for flight training, surveillance and observation. "It had no lights, no radio, no nothing," Willingham says. "It was just a simple airplane, and we were lucky to get it back in those days. It had about an 85 horsepower engine. It was a nice little plane for landing and taking off in tight spaces. You could land it in 100 feet, if you had to, but I had to make sure I had enough room to take off. It took between 300 and 500 feet to take off, especially if you had a passenger in the back."

1947 Aeronca Champion (Courtesy of Adrian Pingstone)

Before taking off, Willingham make a pivotal decision that he regrets to this day. In the rush to get off the ground as quickly as possible and knowing that evidence of the UFO crash would be quickly removed, the pilot decided not to take the time necessary to find a camera to take along on the flight. "We just didn't have the time," Willingham says, "We were racing against the darkness in a plane that had no lights. I didn't have a chance to go anywhere to get a camera. We just got in the airplane and took off."

By the time Willingham eased the Aeronca out onto the runway at the old Corsicana Air Field, it was about 2 p.m. The flight to Langtry, in the slow, little propeller-driven plane was an uncomfortable one for the two men, but they were buoyed by the expectation of possibly finding an answer to the elusive question that had puzzled military flyers for years: what exactly were those things called UFOs? For Robert Willingham, it was a mystery he had wondered about since he was eight years old, when he listened to one of his neighbors in Holliday, Texas, describing a mysterious flying airship that he had seen in the 1930s.Willingham piloted the Aeronca from the plane's front seat, and Perkins sat in the rear seat, where the pilot would normally sit. "It was built to be a trainer," Willingham remembers, "And the pilot is supposed to sit behind, but I flew it from the front."

As the small plane continued heading south, Willingham worried that there would be nothing left to see when they arrived at the crash site. "They usually get that stuff undercover pretty quick," he says.

An Aeronca Champion, with a good tailwind, could fly at about 150 miles per hour and had a range of 460 miles. Willingham recalls that with a stiff tailwind, the Aeronca made the 300 miles to Langtry in about two hours. It was now about 4 p.m., and about three hours had elapsed since Willingham observed the flying object crash-land near Langtry. He circled the Aeronca looking for a nice level place to bring the plane down, and one that had enough space to also allow a take off.

The scene that greeted their eyes was awesome indeed. The UFO had impacted very close to the edge of a flat rocky ledge overlooking the Rio Grande River. It first bounced and then skidded about 300 yards generally toward the south, plowing up a mound of dirt ahead of it as it went along. The main object split into three large sections, and smaller debris was scattered all along the skid line. The top of the object, which was dome-shaped and approximately 12 to 15 feet in diameter, broke off and landed about 50 feet beyond the main body of the UFO. The main section, which originally was a flattened disc between 21 and 25 feet in diameter, broke into two large pieces and many smaller ones.

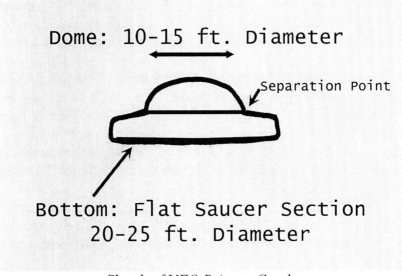

Dome: 10-15 ft. Diameter

Separation Point

Bottom: Flat Saucer Section
20-25 ft. Diameter

Sketch of UFO Prior to Crash

The bottom part of the UFO, ripped into two large sections, was partially embedded against a sand mound, while the dome lay about 50 feet beyond it. Willingham and his partner noted a long plume of shiny metal debris that extended along the long furrow, where the object hit and skidded on the sandy desert soil prior to coming to rest. Judging from the length of the furrow, Willingham guessed that the UFO was traveling "pretty fast" before hitting the ground.

Willingham angled the Aeronca in from the north-northwest and eased it onto the rocky ledge between the crashed UFO and the edge of a small cliff leading down to the Rio Grande. The small plane came to a stop close to where the skid line began, just alongside where the ledge drops off to the river below.

(Photo Courtesy of U.S. Geological Survey)

In an exclusive disclosure for this book, Willingham, using maps from the U.S. Geological Survey and *Google Earth* ™, pinpointed for the authors exactly where the UFO crash site occurred. "It's right there beside that wash that appears on the [satellite] map. Seeing this map has really brought it all back to me. The UFO had stopped right on the edge of that wash." This corresponds with the area marked in the U.S. Geological Survey satellite maps shown in this chapter.

The Mexican soldiers, who had arrived in jeeps and cars, watched with interest as the small plane appeared in the sky from the north, circled, and then touched down near the crashed object that they were guarding. After the plane sputtered to a stop, Willingham, wearing an olive-drab flight suit, and Perkins, wearing coveralls with the words *Electronic Control* on the back, stepped out of the Aeronca and surveyed the remarkable scene before them. They saw close up the long furrow in the sand that had been caused by the skidding fireball, and they could also see the metallic debris that littered the crash site. Immediately after landing, Willingham and Perkins turned the small plane around, facing back to the west, in preparation for take off. Then, the two men quietly walked toward the crashed object, feeling a growing apprehension about the armed Mexican soldiers that guarded the perimeter of the crash site.

Close-up Showing Approximate Skid Path (USGS)

"We landed right there along the river, right across from Judge Roy Bean's place," Willingham says. On that rocky ledge about 150 yards from the river's edge, a sight unlike any he had ever seen greeted the two aviators as they got out of their airplane.

THE CRASHED DISC

As Willingham and Perkins moved along the skid line toward the crashed UFO and the Mexican soldiers that surrounding it, they passed metallic debris of many sizes and shapes. "There were lots of pieces of debris, some little and some large chunks, about as big as a good sofa chair," Willingham remembers.

Artist's Sketch of Crashed UFO Shown on Japanese TV in 1978

To Willingham, it was clear that the Mexicans were not engaged in a retrieval operation. They had no trucks at the scene, only jeeps and cars. There was no effort underway to collect any debris. They did not seem interested in attempting to cool down the still intensely hot UFO. The soldiers seemed content to seal off the crash site and keep civilians safely away from it. More than anything, the Mexicans seemed to be waiting for something. For what, Willingham did not yet know.

"They were just looking at everything," Willingham remembers. "Of course, it was still red hot, and they were staying back from it."

It was at this point that a Langtry resident "paddled" across the shallow waters of the Rio Grande to talk to Willingham and Perkins. The man related his experience of seeing the flaming UFO come streaking across the sky from the north, nearly clipping the top of his house, before zooming across the river and crashing. He told them, "I was working in the backyard, and all of a sudden I saw a fireball come across the sky. It like to scared me to death!"

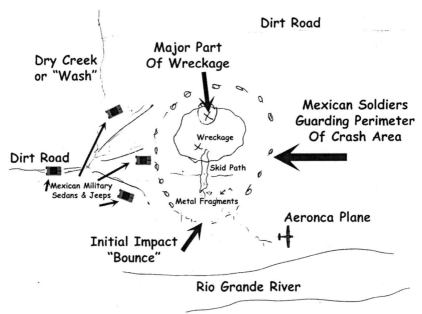

Illustration Based on Willingham's Sketch of Crash Site

Willingham and Perkins then continued following the skid marks toward the object itself, and they noticed the Mexican soldiers stiffen to attention. After the two Americans had walked about 100 yards and were still quite a distance from the crashed disc, one of the soldiers broke from the group and quickly stepped toward them, rifle in his hands.

It became clear to Willingham, who spoke Spanish, that the Mexicans did not welcome their intrusion. "They wouldn't let us anywhere near to it," he recalls. "They were definitely not friendly, especially the officers." He did, however, notice that the soldiers kept eyeing his Air Force attire. It was almost as if they were debating about whether they should allow Willingham onto the scene because of his U.S. military status.

Crash Site with Coordinates Grid (USGS)

Willingham and Perkins took some steps backward but did not leave quite yet. After a bit, Willingham moved over to one of the soldiers and struck up a conversation with him. "I spoke some Spanish, because I took part of my schooling at an Indian school out in New Mexico. When I speak Spanish, it's about half Spanish and half Indian," Willingham says.

Willingham lit up a cigarette and chatted with the Mexican. "Can I have one?" the soldier asked, pointing to Willingham's cigarette.

"You can have the pack," Willingham replied, "We get them for fifty cents down at the base."

One of the Mexican officers, a Lieutenant Martinez from Mexico City, offered to take Willingham closer to the actual impact point. Martinez, who spoke English, told Willingham, "Come on over here. I'll go ahead and take you down there." Perkins, however, was not allowed to accompany them.

Artist's Sketch of Crashed UFO Shown on Japanese TV in 1978

As they approached the UFO, Willingham noticed that a couple of the soldiers were putting their blankets on the strange object in order to warm them up. The soldiers would then cover themselves with the warm blankets to fend off the chilly desert air. Obviously the crashed UFO was still very hot, and Willingham told one of the Mexicans, "Those boys better not grab a hold of any of it [the wreckage], because that stuff is still red hot," Willingham said, as he approached to within 35 or 40 feet of the burning hot object. "I got fairly close, but then they told me, that's as close as you get." Immediately, two soldiers carrying rifles tipped with bayonets blocked his way, and he halted his progress.

Standing within 35 feet of the main wreckage site of the mysterious object, Willingham could see that the UFO had sustained considerable damage, which made its original shape hard to determine. "It [the bottom section] looks oval-like, but it had been broken in two," he recalls. "Because so many pieces had been broken off, I couldn't tell if the object was round or oval."

Mexican Army Officer, Circa 1950

Off in the distance, Willingham could see the dome of the UFO, which had separated during impact. It was more heavily guarded than were the other parts of the craft. Under no circumstances would the Mexicans permit Willingham anywhere near the UFO's dome section. He recalls that he had an urge to go look at the dome, but the soldiers would not allow it.

Martinez, who by this time had been joined by a number of other Mexican officers, told Willingham, "We can't let anyone get close to it. The *American* air force will be here very soon to clean all this up."

"Yes," Willingham said, pointing to his Air Force flight suit, "I'm one of them."

The Mexicans seemed confused and, pointing to the smoldering UFO, one of them asked, "Oh … so what do you want us to do with all this?"

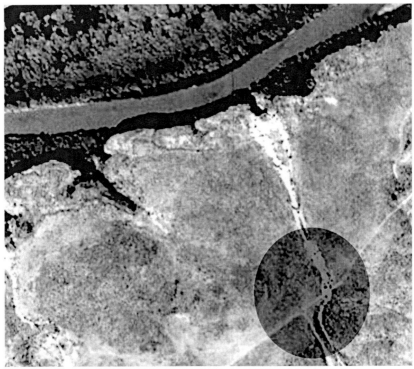

Approximate Location of Main UFO Crash Debris
(Photo Courtesy of U.S. Geological Survey)

At first, Willingham did not know exactly how to respond, but, as he remembered hearing something about the Mexican military keeping UFO wreckage at a secret location near Mexico

City, he said, "Just gather it all up and take it down to Mexico City or wherever it is that you take them."

Another group of officers stepped up and told Willingham that he had to get his plane out of there right away. "Move it right now," one of them told him, "Our boss ["*jefe*"] is on his way here." Willingham says, "I imagine that one of their generals was coming to look over the scene."

The officer's directive was backed up by another show of rifles and bayonets by the surrounding soldiers. This prompted Willingham to retreat and move to where Perkins was standing.

About thirty minutes had passed since they first arrived and they still faced a 330-mile flight. "It's getting close to sundown," Willingham told Perkins. "We better get the heck out of here."

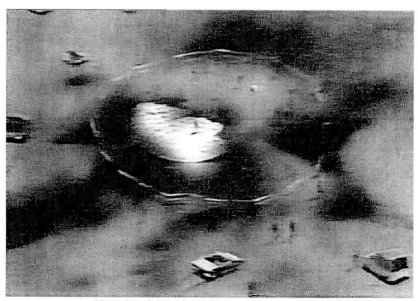

Artist's Sketch of Crashed Saucer Section (Japan TV)

Taking in the surreal scene one last time, Willingham was again struck by the fact that the Mexicans were making no effort to retrieve the wreckage and move it out. "They weren't trying to haul away any of the stuff," he remembers. And then there was the cryptic statement about the American air force being on the way to deal with the debris.

Also, Willingham noticed that, in addition to the squadron of enlisted men and several officers at the scene, a number of other official-looking persons were hanging around the site. Willingham can describe them only as Mexican "government officials." It is possible that these men were somehow involved in making sure that nothing was disturbed prior to the arrival of an American retrieval team.

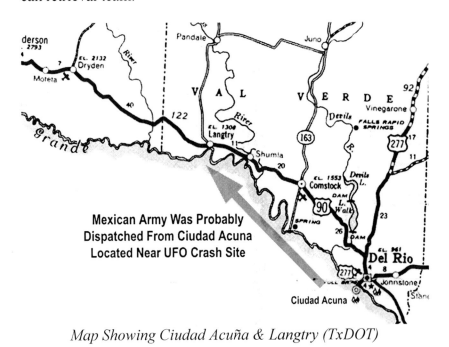

Map Showing Ciudad Acuña & Langtry (TxDOT)

The Mexican military personnel on the scene probably came from the army base at Ciudad Acuña, located over 100 miles away. The region of Mexico where the crash occurred is extremely desolate, mountainous, and difficult to reach by land vehicle. Acuña is the nearest Mexican city of any significant size, situated just across the international bridge from Del Rio. The terrain between the UFO crash site and Ciudad Acuña represents one of the roughest stretches of desert and mountains in the whole of Coahuila state. "I have no idea where they came from," says Willingham. "Many of those little border towns have a platoon of soldiers." Reflecting a moment, he adds that the enlisted men had on a light tan khaki uniform, while the officers wore a dark green uniform. Since he was unfamiliar with Mexican military license plates, the jeeps and other vehicles yielded no clue as to the squadron's origin.

1978 Japanese TV Sketch of U.S. Recovery Team Operations

Since the army base at Ciudad Acuña is the only major military installation in Coahuila, it seems likely to have been the point of origin for the soldiers who first arrived at the crash site. Ciudad Acuña, whose current population is over 126,000, had the best infrastructure for communications and other military logistics. Ciudad Acuña is the site of one of eleven Mexican military garrisons along the international border with the United States. If the U.S. Air Force had indeed contacted the Mexican military asking for their assistance in guarding a downed "aircraft" until they arrived, it is likely that the Americans contacted the army base in Ciudad Acuña, which is a stone's throw away from Laughlin Air Force Base in Del Rio. Obviously, word would have arrived down the chain of command to Laughlin, from where it was relayed to the Mexican army base in Ciudad Acuña.

The Mexicans took no aircraft or trucks to the UFO crash site, and certainly, they did not intend to carry out a recovery operation. As they told Willingham, their function was simply to guard the crashed object until the "American air force" arrived to deal with it. As for how the Mexicans learned of the UFO crash in such a remote area of their country, Willingham says, "The way I got it later was that the U.S. Air Force had contacted the Mexicans and told them that it [the object] was coming down. That's why they [the Mexicans] arrived there first."

The recovery of the crashed UFO may have been handled by an elite crash-recovery unit out of Fort Belvoir, Virginia, that operated in the 1950s under the codename *Operation Blue Fly*. The unit, whose history will be more thoroughly explored in a later chapter, was part of the 4602nd Air Intelligence Service Squadron.

A retired Army officer who claims to have taken part in crash recovery operations told the authors of this book, "When there's a report of a craft going down, they [defense intelligence agents] are normally given a heads up, saying, something is going to happen within a certain period of time. They say, we need to know if you get any reports of little green men, flying saucers, landings of flying saucers, or anything of this sort. We need to know about that. They then begin sending spot reports - that is, flash immediate reports - stating that local newspapers are carrying reports of this and that, a report of a flaming object landing on the ground near such-and-such village, etc. Immediately, you have teams ready to go into play. At some point, and that may take several hours, there will be a three-man team sent from Fort Belvoir, Virginia, immediately to that location. They are the ones who will be in charge. They will be in civilian clothes. You won't know what rank they are. Prior to that happening, you will also have a quick-response team that goes out there, and they're well trained and well equipped, and it's going to be an N.B.C. [Nuclear, Biological, and Chemical] team. You have two teams that are going to respond. A-team is situated to where they are in close proximity, to where they can be there within two hours. B-team has to be there within four hours. You can draw on the resources of the nearest military installations to provide for security at that area."

The retired officer says that the teams' initial objective is to move the crash debris to a safe location. "Now, the first thing you do if this object or material goes down in a foreign country is take that material or object to what we call a safe haven area, which is not necessarily a military base. This move can be accomplished by aircraft, or it can be accomplished by a truck convoy. With a truck convoy, you're provided with a toll-free number should any of the vehicles break down. Most of the time it's not obvious that the convoy is under armed guard, but *it is* under armed guard."

Sketch of U.S. Recovery Team Operations (Japan TV)

Before the debris was hauled away in the Langtry crash, however, it was witnessed by Robert Willingham. And, although the Mexican soldiers did not allow him to get very close to the crashed disc, he did see enough to conclude that the object was not of this earth.

THE RETURN

As Willingham and Perkins moved away from the heavily guarded UFO and headed for their airplane, Willingham suddenly decided he was not leaving without some evidence of what he had seen. Waiting until he was almost back to the plane, Willingham nonchalantly bent over and picked up one of the many shiny pieces of metal that littered the ground at the crash site. The metal fragment was still extremely hot, prompting Willingham to wrap it up in his handkerchief and put it in the pocket of his flight jacket. He remembers, "I was even worried that it might start my jacket on fire." Although he did not realize it at the time, that small piece of smoldering metallic debris would change his life forever.

Photo of Aeronca from Willingham's Photo Collection

Feeling the pressure of the Mexicans' admonition to leave quickly, Willingham and Perkins boarded the Aeronca Champion and taxied the small plane to a point several hundred feet away, close to where it had originally touched down. Turning the plane around to point east, Willingham started his run across the rocky ledge and lifted the plane off on a heading to the east-northeast. The time was approximately 4:30 p.m.

With darkness approaching, a strong headwind opposing them, and their fuel running low, the flight back home proved slow and arduous. Willingham had to put the plane down on a small airstrip near Waco, Texas, in order to refuel for the remaining distance to Corsicana. As he stood in that lonely airfield in central Texas, Willingham fingered the small piece of metal in his pocket and wondered what it was. Was it possible that he was holding a fragment of an extraterrestrial spaceship? The awesomeness of the moment descended upon him.

The Trip Back to Corsicana (UT-Austin Libraries)

64

About six hours after leaving Langtry, the Aeronca touched down in Corsicana, and the two aviators finally had a chance to go home and rest.

On the following day, Willingham returned to Carswell Air Force Base and prepared a full written report about his incident. He remembers filling out the paperwork fully and in great detail. Asked where the report might be today, Willingham shrugs and says, "Probably stored away in a box somewhere among a million other government files." He remembers that at the time he was filling out the report, he viewed it as a rather routine task, such as he had carried out many times before, despite the fact that so much about this incident was so strange.

After he filled out the paperwork, a secretary typed it and forwarded it to the commander of the Air Force Reserve unit, a Colonel Miller. Sometime afterward, Miller summoned him into his office for a verbal debriefing about the incident and about his report. Present in the room along with Miller were two other pilots who had also seen the UFO and a secretary that was presumably there to take notes. One of the pilots, George Smithson, had served overseas with Willingham during World War II, and the two men remained in touch for years after leaving military service.

Smithson and the other pilot admitted seeing an extremely bright light traveling at a high rate of speed across the sky. "They had seen the bright lights, and that's all," Willingham remembers. Smithson and the other man also stated that from their vantage point they did not witness the 90-degree turn seen by Willingham. Nor did they see the object begin to descend and eventually fall out of the sky along the Texas-Mexico border. This makes sense, however, since Willingham's was the only aircraft that chased the UFO as it moved south away from the point of the initial sighting.

Then, Willingham told his astonishing story in great detail, as the commander and the others listened quietly and took notes. "They didn't really say anything or respond in any way," Willingham remembers. "But, this is normal. The way it works is that they take your report and what you say during the interview and discuss it with other officers later. Then, they get back to you if they feel you did something wrong or if you need to know something else."

AI FORM 112—PART II
APPROVED 1 JUNE 1949

AIR INTELLIGENCE INFORMATION REPORT

| Laredo Air Force Base, Texas | ATRC IR-PP-52 | 2 | 3 |

1. On the night of 4 December 1952, 1st Lt Robert O. Arnold was flying locally in a T-28 type aircraft for the purpose of completing AFR 60-2 requirements. After flying in the local area for approximately two hours, Lt Arnold returned to the airfield to enter traffic and land. Student training in T-33 Jet aircraft was in progress and the landing period was in session. Lt Arnold received this information from the tower and therefore remained aloft until the landing period was over so that he might enter normal traffic and land.

2. While waiting for permission from the tower to land, Lt Arnold circled the field in a counter clockwise manner and observed the Jet aircraft in the pattern and landing from an altitude of 6000'. After approximately 45 minutes of holding aloft, Lt Arnold ascertained there were only three Jet aircraft remaining in traffic. A surveillance of the immediate area around the field to see if any other aircraft remained aloft was made by Lt Arnold to determine how much longer he would be required to hold before landing. It was at this time he noticed a rapidly moving bluish light at approximate traffic altitude (1500' to 2000'). It was approximately 8 o'clock

Typical 1950s Report Based on Pilot Sighting (Blue Book Archive)

Meanwhile, the crew of the B-47 that Willingham was escorting on the day of the UFO incident received a separate debriefing upon arriving in the state of Washington. Whatever they were told caused them to remain silent about the encounter for the rest of their lives, as far as Willingham knows. He did try to make contact with members of the B-47 crew over the years but was never able to locate them.

At this point, Willingham did not feel especially anxious about what had occurred to him. It seemed to him that he was just going through the routine motions of his duties as a pilot and a reservist. Little did he realize that the information he had given in both his written report and during his interview would soon come back to haunt him.

Curious to find out what action was taken about his UFO sighting, Willingham went to talk to Colonel Miller some time later. When he asked if Miller would help him find out more about the case, the colonel abruptly informed him, "No, I won't be here tomorrow, I'm leaving today. I'm retired and gone, and you just might as well do the same."

Willingham also received disturbing phone calls from other USAF personnel. "Don't say anything about what you saw down on the border," He was instructed by a general who worked with Air Force intelligence. In a separate call from a major in intelligence, Willingham was warned of "consequences" if he spoke publicly about what he witnessed.

Interestingly, Willingham's companion on the trip to Langtry, Jack Perkins, slipped quietly under the military's radar screen when the cover-up began to unfold. Because nobody knew that Perkins went along on the flight and because Willingham never revealed his identity until after Perkins passed away in 2002, he was effectively shielded from the type of pressure to which Willingham was subjected. "As far as they knew, I flew down there by myself," Willingham says.

It was lucky for Perkins that Willingham protected him.

10

THE ARTIFACT

Before leaving the site of the UFO crash, Robert Willingham bent over and picked up a shiny piece of metallic debris. "I saw a little piece of metal lying there, and I picked it up," He recalls. "It was still hot." Turning to Perkins, he said, "We'll just take this along with us. See what it's made of."

Sketch of UFO Debris Drawn in 1978 by Willingham

In the hours and days following the incident, Willingham closely examined the strange artifact that he recovered from the crash site. As a result of his father's work as an oil company metallurgist and his own interest in metallurgy, Willingham was extremely interested in finding out more about the strange material. But, he had no time for a careful examination at the scene of the crash. That would have to wait.

"I just wrapped my handkerchief around it and stuck it in a pocket of my flight suit," Willingham says. The unearthly piece of metal was "about the size of a man's hand" and was half an inch thick. Years later, in 1978, he drew the sketch shown above, displaying a curved piece of metal with holes in the front. Although rigid and unyielding, it was extremely light. It had the look of stainless steel but had a grayish silver coloration. "In a way it looked like magnesium steel, but it had a lot of carbon in it." Also, it had several small, precisely crafted holes in a honeycomb pattern on one side of it. "We figured it was to dissipate the heat," Willingham says. "Also, on the left side of my sketch, where you see ridges, these were kind of jagged, as if this piece had been broken off from a larger object."

There were no symbols, numbers, or written characters on it, unlike the metallic debris found after the 1947 crash of a UFO near Roswell, New Mexico. Also, the piece clearly had been detached from a larger mechanism, because it gave the appearance of being part of something else. "We don't know what part of the object it came from."

"It wasn't very big," Willingham recalls. "What really got me is that it wouldn't burn and it was honeycombed with holes. Being a metallurgist myself, I've never seen anything like it. The outside was kind of a dark gray and the inside of it was kind of orange colored."

When he first picked the metal up at the crash site in Langtry, it seemed warm to the touch. Over the course of the next several hours, it had cooled. To Willingham, something about the metal's appearance and characteristics puzzled him greatly. He decided to study it more closely and run a series of tests on it to determine its make-up.

Inspecting it further, Willingham focused on the strange "honeycomb" design to the metal, which led him to conclude that it was of intelligent manufacture. He later said, "It looked like something that was made, because it was honeycombed. You know how you would make a metal that would cool faster." In some UFO cases, witnesses have claimed to find metals with strange properties, including "memory metals." Memory metals are said to automatically revert to their original shape even when twisted, crinkled, or otherwise deformed. Willingham does not know if his piece had memory metal characteristics, as it was too thick and rigid to bend or twist.

Close Up of Willingham's 1978 Sketch

He decided to test the metal's hardness and melting point by using a cutting torch on it. This is where the big surprise came. After subjecting the metal fragment to the intense heat of the cutting torch for an extended period, Willingham determined that, although the metal became hot, it would not melt. He observed, "I tried to heat it with a cutting torch. It just wouldn't melt."

Willingham's impromptu cutting torch experiment was enough to convince him that the metal fragment was not of the Earth. "A cutting torch burns anywhere from 3,200 to 3,800 degrees Fahrenheit, and it would make the metal hot, but it wouldn't even start the metal to yield," he said.

A Cutting Torch in Use (U.S. National Park Service)

"The cutting torch made the metal turn slightly blue for a while, but it did no lasting damage," Willingham says. He performed other tests in an effort to cut or deform the metal, but nothing would affect it. "We tried a cutting torch, grinders, and everything else, but nothing would even touch it."

He remembers having the artifact in his possession for three or four days. Unfortunately, he became so focused on running physical various tests on the metal that it never occurred to him to take any photographs of the object, another decision that he now greatly regrets.

Determined to discover more about the mysterious fragment in his possession, Willingham decided that he needed access to a laboratory facility that had more sophisticated equipment for subjecting the metal to additional tests that could determine for certain its composition and point of origin.

Willingham arranged to take the metal fragment to a Marine Corps metallurgy laboratory in Hagerstown, Maryland. He and his navigator, whose name he no longer remembers, flew up to Maryland to deliver it to the lab.

Air Force Metallurgy Lab (USAF Photo)

Arriving at the facility in Maryland, Willingham and his navigator met with a metallurgist there, a Marine Corps major. "The major took it right to the lab, and he kept looking at it. He said, Boy, I've never seen anything like that. He did the same tests I did. He took a grinder and tried to grind it and everything else. Finally, he said, Man, that's good stuff!"

The metallurgist assured Willingham that more extensive tests would be conducted and that the findings would be available in a day or two. Anxious to know more about the metal, Willingham gave the major his telephone number, stressing that although he had to return to his base in Texas, he wanted to be contacted as soon as the test results were ready. Willingham wrote down the metallurgist's name so that he could ask for him directly in the future.

A day later, back in Texas, Willingham received a cryptic phone call from the major at the metallurgy lab. "I'm sorry, but we have to move out of the building," the major said, sounding hurried and anxious. "Someday I'll find you." The phone line clicked off.

Later, when Willingham contacted the lab and asked to speak to the major, he was told that no such person worked there or had ever worked there. Also, nobody knew anything about the mysterious metal fragment that Willingham had dropped off there only a few days before. There was no record of the metal ever having arrived there or of any tests ever having been conducted on it. Angry and extremely troubled, Willingham traveled back to Maryland to find out what happened, but "I couldn't find him [the major], couldn't find the piece of metal, no notification that it was ever there or anything like that." He tried to pursue the matter through the facility's chain of command but was told that not only was there no information that anyone could disclose to him, but that it would be in his best interest not to mention the metal fragment anymore to anyone. "That was it," Willingham says, remembering that the game was up for him at that point.

Willingham Holds His Sketch During 1978 TV Interview

The strange and wonderful artifact that he suspected might not be of this earth had been snatched away from him and taken out of his reach. In addition to an overpowering sense of loss and sadness, he now also began to feel something else – danger. The warning that he had been given about not mentioning the metal was only the first of several others he would soon receive. Obviously, the lid of secrecy that has always surrounded major UFO cases was about to come slamming down on Willingham and his story.

During a 1978 interview for Japanese television, Willingham first unveiled the sketch he drew of the metallic UFO debris. To this day, Willingham realizes that the strange properties of the unearthly metal he found that day along the Rio Grande River form the key to unraveling the whole mystery. He admits that skeptics can argue that what he saw while flying in his F-86 may not have been a flying saucer, and others may say that what he saw crashed along the river was not one, either. But, as an amateur metallurgist himself, he knew that the strange piece of metal could not be explained away so easily. Asked what he would tell someone who suggests that what he saw in Langtry was a crashed missile or experimental aircraft, he quickly replies, "Might have been so, if it wasn't for that piece of metal. That piece of metal told me that it was something else, because I'm a pretty good metallurgist myself. It sure wasn't your common piece of metal."

"I've been welding since I was nine years old," he continues. "My daddy was a blacksmith and a welder. I learned to acetylene weld when I was about nine or ten, and I worked with a lot of different metals."

The persons or agencies interested in keeping UFOs hidden from the public had to make certain that Willingham's metal fragment disappeared, along with the metallurgist who took it from him. The steps taken to relieve him of the metal were immediate and well planned.

Skeptics might argue that the intelligence services would not be all that interested in a metal fragment reportedly from a UFO. Yet, several recently declassified government documents suggest otherwise. In one of the first documented cases of UFO debris falling into the hands of the U.S. government, a 1948 Army report that was declassified in 1998 contains information about a metallic chunk that came from an "alleged flying saucer." Photographs of a small teardrop-shaped piece of metallic debris were released under a Freedom of Information Act (FOIA) request seeking all documents containing the phrase "flying saucer."

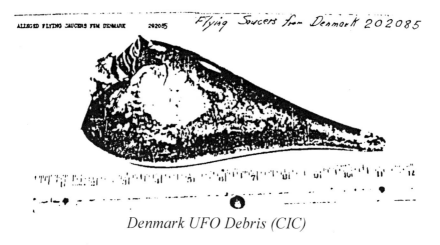

Denmark UFO Debris (CIC)

Labeled U.S. Army Counter Intelligence Corps (CIC) document number 202085, the release contains only photographs of the object, which was said to have come from Denmark. No narrative is provided in this document, and no additional mention is made about the metal's origin, the circumstances surrounding its finding, or its current whereabouts. However, in 2003, a former U.S. Department of Defense physicist, Dr. Gilbert Jordan, came forward with a stunning disclosure: "I am going on record that I have seen, at an Army facility, an object similar to that described in C.I.C. number 202085...." Jordan's statement appears in a 2003 news release written by Larry Cekander of the *Museum of the Unexplained*.

In the statement, Jordan also compares the Denmark object to another piece of debris that was found by eyewitness Bob White following a UFO encounter near Grand Junction, Colorado, in 1985. White and a female traveling companion saw two huge bright lights that looked like long horizontal bars in the night sky. Before zooming away, one of the objects ejected a piece of molten metallic debris that struck the ground a short distance away from where White and his companion stood.

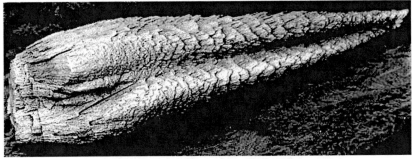

UFO Debris Found by Bob White

At first, the object was intensely hot and, only after it cooled, was White able to investigate it closely. About 7 ½ inches in length, the teardrop-shaped object had "unusual feathering or scales flowing toward the tale," according to an article at AboveTopSecret.com. It weighs less than two pounds. The similarity to the Denmark UFO object is striking, as pointed out by physicist Jordan, who said he "told Bob White that it [the Denmark object] was a lightweight object, but smaller than that of his object."

After keeping the discovery to himself for over ten years for fear of being branded a "UFO nut," White finally disclosed his finding in 1996 and had the object looked at by a number of metallurgic laboratories. Tests determined that the object was composed mostly of aluminum and silicone and contained no unknown elements; however, the metal did possess a number of strange properties suggesting it was not manufactured on Earth. After testing by the Los Alamos National Laboratory in 1996, the subsequent report contained 19 references to the metal debris as an "unknown object of unknown origin."

To deepen the mystery, bubble chamber radiation tests conducted in 2006 detected the presence of neutron radiation within the object – another anomaly. Neutron radiation is the type of ionizing radiation most commonly found in nuclear reactors and nuclear bombs. The so-called *neutron bomb* is based on the emission of massive amounts of neutron radiation with little heat or light, thus killing all living creatures in the blast area but leaving buildings and other structures undisturbed.

Location of Fallen UFO Fragment (CIA Map)

In addition to these UFO fragments, a recently declassified U.S. government document also reveals another incident where a metallic fragment was recovered at the site of a UFO crash. Released under the Freedom of Information Act (FOIA), an April CIA 1966 memo, which is titled "Exploitation of Metallic Fragment From Unidentified Flying Object," states the following: "On file in CIA Library is an exploitation report on a metallic fragment approximately 2" x 2" x 1", recovered near Kerekere, Republic of the Congo."

"The fragment was recovered by ground search after a UFO fell to earth in the area. The report concludes that the fragment was originally part of an electrical component and was constructed of 0.010-inch thick silicon-steel laminate."

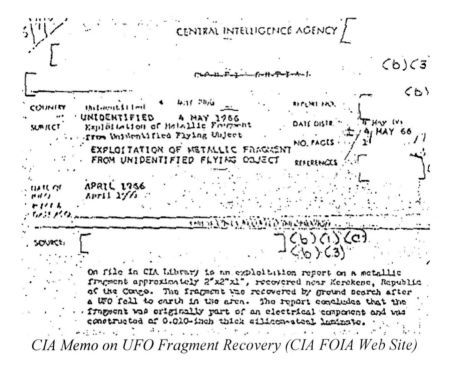

CIA Memo on UFO Fragment Recovery (CIA FOIA Web Site)

The "exploitation report" to which the CIA memo refers has also been recently released under FOIA by the National Security Agency (NSA). The NSA release of the document is of such poor quality that much of it cannot be read; however, the readable parts state the following: "Exploitation Report – Fragment, Metal, Recovered in the Republic of the Congo. Origin Believed to Be an Unidentified Flying Object (Country Unidentified). The purpose of this report is to present the results of the exploitation of a metallic fragment recovered near the town of Kerekere in the Republic of the Congo. Fragment recovery was the result of a ground level search which was conducted after an unidentified flying object exploded and fell to earth in the area. The sighting and recovery took place sometime between 10 and 15 October 1965. Other than a reported east-to-west flight for the UFO, specific observation and recovery details are lacking. Details concerning the exact location and characteristics of impact are unknown; however, the appearance of the fragment indicated exposure to high temperatures..."

The report continues, "The fragment was originally [probably] an electrical component... 0.10-inch thick silicon steel laminate stacked on a central soft ... core or shaft. Materials, processes, dimensions, etc., as such, prevent determination of exact origin (country). Surface appearance and microstructure of the speciman indicates exposure to temperatures in excess of 2,500 degrees F." Among the metals in the fragment were manganese, silicon, nickel, chromium, and molybdenum.

Robert Willingham is convinced that somewhere in a high security area, perhaps at a secret military facility, the piece of UFO metal that he collected in Langtry, Texas, in 1955, underwent similar, thorough "exploitation testing." Somewhere a detailed, highly classified report exists with descriptions, diagrams, charts, and conclusions. He would dearly love to see that someday, but, at age 82, he realizes that his days are growing short.

In UFO cases like that of Robert Willingham, evidence is quickly extracted and hidden from public view, and people who saw or handled the evidence find themselves transferred out and isolated from contact with others who saw the evidence. One UFO investigator cites the example of a UFO landing in Lamboy Woods, Germany, where several U.S. military police officers witnessed the event. "Within 24 hours, every MP that was close enough to see anything was sent to the four corners of the earth. That way, they can never get together to compare notes. It affects you deeply. If you try to tell anyone, you have no one that was there with you, and so nobody believes you, and you become a fine candidate to be sent up for a psychological evaluation."

In Willingham's case, evidence and witnesses vanished with breathtaking quickness. It seems likely that most of the other pilots who were flying with him on the day of the initial UFO sighting were transferred out, as he later had trouble finding and talking to them. The metallurgist at the lab in Maryland was hastily transferred elsewhere. The crash scene was quickly scrubbed clean. And, the retrieved piece of metal was made to disappear.

Sketch of UFO Debris Drawn in 1978 by Willingham

Asked where Willingham's mysterious metal might have ended up, one investigator told us, "It probably wound up at some university that is contracted by the U.S. government under DARPA [Defense Advance Research Projects Agency] to do research and development on it. See, what we do is seed this information out to laboratories and to universities under contract. It makes things easier because it is no longer subject to the Freedom of Information Act, because even though the government owns it, proprietary ownership transfers to the university or private industry that has contracts with the federal government and has been cleared to work on classified projects. So what you have done is removed it to where it is no longer subject to government scrutiny, except by a small, select, hand-picked group of people with a specific need to know."

THE ARTIFACT

In an interesting footnote to the story, about two years after he dropped off the metal fragment for testing at the lab in Maryland, Willingham received a mysterious letter in the mail. It had no return address and was not signed. The letter said simply, "I don't know what kind of metal it is, but I've never tested anything like it before." Willingham is convinced that the note came from the metallurgist to whom he delivered the strange metallic fragment.

11

THE COVER-UP

Even as Robert Willingham resumed his normal routine in the days after witnessing the UFO crash, it became clear that a high-level cover-up of the incident was already underway. For the U.S. intelligence operatives involved, the Willingham case presented several unique challenges. Sightings of UFOs were common during this era and could be dealt with. Cover stories, threats, and intimidation could be successfully employed to keep witnesses, especially military personnel, from talking. Documents and records could be destroyed, as in Ruppelt's 1952 case of another F-86 encounter with a UFO. However, in the Willingham incident, an artifact had been removed from the crash site, and it had to be retrieved.

Once Willingham turned over his metallic fragment to the military lab, it was made to disappear from the face of the earth, along with the person who had received it. Clearly, someone had made the connection between the mysterious piece of metal and Willingham's UFO sighting a few days earlier.

In addition to the snatching of the artifact, a lid of secrecy was also coming down on everyone involved in the sighting of the UFO and, especially, on Willingham. He recalls that shortly after the incident, all the aviators who flew that day were instructed, "Don't say one word about any of it."

Willingham himself was contacted by a general working for Air Force intelligence, whose name he remembers only as "Iron" White. "He told me to keep my mouth shut and be mum about it, or there would be consequences." He recalls White saying, "The little incident you had down here on the border – you will not say anything to anybody about it. Do you understand?"

TOP SECRET

THIS IS A COVER SHEET

FOR CLASSIFIED INFORMATION

ALL INDIVIDUALS HANDLING THIS INFORMATION ARE REQUIRED TO PROTECT IT FROM UNAUTHORIZED DISCLOSURE IN THE INTEREST OF THE NATIONAL SECURITY OF THE UNITED STATES.

HANDLING, STORAGE, REPRODUCTION AND DISPOSITION OF THE ATTACHED DOCUMENT WILL BE IN ACCORDANCE WITH APPLICABLE EXECUTIVE ORDER(S), STATUTE(S) AND AGENCY IMPLEMENTING REGULATIONS.

Typical Cover Sheet for Top Secret Files (Wikipedia.org)

Willingham told White that he understood, but also asked whether he could talk if commanded to do so by a general. The intelligence officer replied, "You will tell *nobody*."

The same directive was delivered to him in a telephone call from another intelligence operative, a "Major Sealton." The message was equally blunt and threatening: "Don't say anything about what you saw. If you do, there will be consequences."

Realizing that the door of secrecy would soon close tightly, Willingham at first resisted. He paid a visit to the radar room at Carswell to ask if they had picked anything up on radar on the day of the encounter. He was met with blank stares. "They said they hadn't picked anything up."

Within two weeks of the UFO encounter, Willingham made a flight down to Langtry, where he hoped to find some evidence of what he had seen on the day of the incident. "I was just getting some flying time in," He remembers, "We were required to get at least four hours a week. The first thing that hit my mind was to go down there and see if it was still there."

Rio Grande River at Langtry (2007 by Noe Torres)

As he circled the crash scene in his airplane, the sinking realization struck him that the entire site had been gone through with a fine toothcomb. "There wasn't a thing left out there anywhere," he sighs. "It's likely that all of the metal fragments were radioactive, and because of that, they were very easy to locate, even if they were buried underground. I've heard that when cases like this happen, they [the team sent to clean up the area] are very thorough."

The curtain of secrecy had been drawn tightly shut. The eyewitnesses had been commanded not to talk. The evidence had been stolen away from Willingham. The crash site had been completely wiped clean. The incident was made to appear as though it had never happened. Only a careful study of other similar cases during the same time period might lead to insights about what was really going on.

Over the years, previously classified documents have surfaced that may shed light on what was going on behind the scenes in military intelligence at this time. A recently declassified National Security Agency (NSA) memo could be of particular significance. Sometime in the summer of 1955, the commander of the Air Force's security service in San Antonio, Texas, suddenly became interested in UFO cases involving B-47 aircraft. He seemed specifically interested in UFO sightings around military installations in the northwestern U.S., near western Canada and Alaska.

Coincidentally, Willingham says that the UFO he encountered had first been spotted by the Distant Early Warning (DEW) radar system in western Canada, as it flew rapidly to the south, eventually reaching Texas and crashing along the border with Mexico. Interestingly, the NSA files reveal several other UFO encounters with military aircraft, including B-47s, during the same time period that Willingham said he had his.

As a result of the request from Air Force Security in Texas, Captain Laddie Marin of the Air Force Special Security Office at the headquarters of the Northeast Air Command (NEAC) in New York responded with 26 pages of information. Copies of the documents were also forwarded to the director of the National Security Agency.

Although the original request for the information has not been released, Marin's response mentions it, stating, "Following is more detailed information on sightings in the NEAC area in June and July as requested in your message."

Marin wrote, "Enclosures 1, 2, 3, and 4 are detailed reports prepared by Watch Division, NEAC, on the 1 to 8 July sightings made by RB-47 crews. D/I NEAC has not correlated these sightings with any known activity."

The Marin letter clearly indicates that someone with Air Force Security in Texas was very interested in encounters involving UFOs and B-47 aircraft, such as the one that

Willingham was escorting in his F-86 on the day of his sighting. Marin attached documentation relating to several B-47 UFO sightings that happened in June and July of 1955.

AIR FORCE SPECIAL SECURITY OFFICE
Headquarters, Northeast Air Command
APO 862 New York, N.Y.

SSO   18 July 1955

SUBJECT: (UNCLASSIFIED) UFOB -NEAC Area

TO: Commander
         USAF Security Service
         San Antonio, Texas

1. Reference to SSO NEAC message, Cite SONEC-13, DTG 0512072 July and your message Cite CCP-X5547, DTG 1223112 July 1955. Following is more detailed information on sighting in the NEAC area in June and July as requested in your message.

Portion of NEAC Letter (NSA FOIA Web Site)

On June 1, an RB-47 flying in the area of Devon Island in Canada made radar contact with a UFO for nearly an hour. The unidentified object, at one point, closed to within 6,000 yards of the aircraft.

On June 3, the crew of another RB-47 made visual contact with a glistening silver metallic object near Melville Island, Canada. Contact was maintained for about nine minutes before the UFO zoomed away at a very high rate of speed.

On June 7, near Alaska's Eielson Air Force Base, an RB-47 made electronic contact with a strange object hovering at about 3,500 yards. No further information about the contact was available.

On June 8, yet another RB-47 made visual and electronic contact with an "unknown aircraft" near Bathurst Island in Canada. Marin's letter then concludes with information about additional sightings in Newfoundland and in Panama.

It seems possible that Air Force Security was looking up other UFO sightings with similar characteristics to the Willingham case. They were perhaps looking for ways to dispose of the case, burying it away from public sight, building up a cover story.

With UFO secrecy extending to the highest levels of government, it is doubtful that Robert Willingham could have accomplished very much even if he had spoken out right away in 1955 about what happened to him, instead of waiting for over a decade. The military's cover-up job is simplified, many investigators argue, because society has been conditioned to disbelieve the notion that UFOs are real and are not of the earth. One UFO researcher told us, "A person has a UFO incident. Now he goes and tells people, hey, this happened. I had this UFO land right in front of me on the highway, and a couple of these real gray guys got out. Suddenly, people are standing back and saying, well, I believe you saw something, but until I see something like that, I'm not going to believe it. He doesn't understand why they won't believe him, and yet the day before yesterday, he was in the same category as the people who won't believe. Now he's had the experience, and now he believes. When it comes to the UFO situation, that's exactly what you're confronted with."

Once the military has removed the hard evidence, debriefed witnesses, and applied a cover story, what remains is simple hearsay of a kind that most people will shy away from. This was the predicament that Willingham found himself in after the UFO incident that suddenly changed his life.

With the security lid slamming down upon him, Willingham grew increasingly isolated and uncertain about his future. He decided to speak no more about the case, and from 1955 until approximately 1967, he did not tell a soul. He also kept no written notes. Unfortunately, during this time period, the head injury that he suffered in Korea in 1950 caused him further health problems. Suddenly, the details about what he saw seemed to be slipping away.

12

CONSEQUENCES

In about 1967, Robert Willingham decided to "cut it loose" and begin speaking about his UFO encounter. He mentioned his strange experience to a reporter for a small weekly newspaper in Pennsylvania, where he was stationed at the time, still in the Air Force Reserve. Interest in UFOs had been stirred up in Pennsylvania following the reported crash of a UFO in the woods near Kecksburg, Pennsylvania, in 1965. Working with the area's Civil Air Patrol, Willingham ran into a reporter who was looking into UFO sightings reported by several Civil Air Patrol pilots in Pennsylvania.

UFO investigator W. Todd Zechel ran across the newspaper clipping ten years later, in 1977. Zechel told the authors of this book, "I first came across Willingham in mid-1977 while working in New York City as a technical consultant for a film company. An article in a Mechanicsburg, Pennsylvania, shopper newspaper, of which I had obtained a copy, about the local Civil Air Patrol chapter, of which Willingham was a member, and the UFO sightings that happened during CAP searches, reported that Willingham 'had seen one [UFO] crashing in Mexico....' A local NICAP [National Investigations Committee on Aerial Phenomena] member had clipped the article out and mailed it into NICAP headquarters, circa 1967. But NICAP had not followed up on the story. Upon meeting Willingham, it became clear he was unsure of the date or location of the supposed crashed saucer event, nor had he observed any U.S. forces recovering it."

After speaking to Zechel, Willingham also filed a brief affidavit about the case with NICAP, although he now admits that the statement had some flaws. For example, it did not mention a date, which led some UFO researchers to attempt to assign a

date of December 1950 to the case. That date does not work because at the time, Willingham was serving in Korea. Also, in the
NICAP affidavit, Willingham states that he was flying an F-94,
although he is now certain it was an F-86. "I flew both of those
planes, but the F-94 is a two-seater, and I'm certain I was alone
in an F-86 when this happened," Willingham says. A couple of
slight inaccuracies have, over the years, thrown many investigators for a loop. In providing the information for this book,
Willingham is revealing, for the first time, the fully detailed account of the incident to the best of his recollection, after having
spent many years thinking and reflecting on his life and experiences.

Willingham, Circa Mid-1960s

One year after filing the NICAP affidavit, Willingham
agreed to tell his story to a Japanese television production crew
that was putting together a documentary about significant UFO
cases in the U.S. Willingham spent several days with the Japa-

nese TV crew, retracing his movements during the UFO incident. Among the locations visited by the crew were: Carswell Air Force Base; Langtry, Texas; Ciudad Acuna, Mexico; and the actual site where Willingham saw the UFO crash. Willingham recalls that the TV crew put together about ten hours worth of video, although the final segment that ran on Japanese television in 1978 was only about thirty minutes in length.

Willingham Appears in 1978 Japanese TV Documentary

Beginning in the late 1970s, Willingham developed a close relationship with Zechel and, after the 1978 Japanese TV documentary, held back on releasing very much additional information to others. Seemingly, Zechel intended to write a book comprising a comprehensive study of Willingham's UFO encounter. Unfortunately, Zechel never wrote the book, as he passed away in November 2006.

Despite Willingham's initial confusion about some of the dates and other details, Zechel stated, "I found Willingham to be a credible source to the extent most everything he told me checked out. Plus, he never tried to embellish or add things to the story he didn't see or know."

After Willingham told his story to the reporter in Pennsylvania in about 1967, the "consequences" he had been warned about seemed to be put into effect against him. When he retired from the military in 1971 or 72, he was told that he was being denied a pension. "I went to apply for my pension," Willingham remembers, "And they told me, you don't have one."

Although the military told him that his pension denial was due to other factors, Willingham immediately suspected that the truth was somewhat more sinister. "Of course, they didn't tell me that it was because of what I said, but I figured it out. Twenty six years of service went down the drain just like that."

Willingham (right) During 1978 Interview with Japanese TV

It is important to note that Willingham has profited almost nothing over the years from his UFO story. He has never written a book, and in agreeing to be interviewed for this book, he expressed no interest in being compensated in any manner. In truth, telling his story has brought him much pain but very little gain. "I did an interview with a Dallas television station, and they promised me $400 but never paid me a cent," he recalls. "But that's fine. I'm not looking for money."

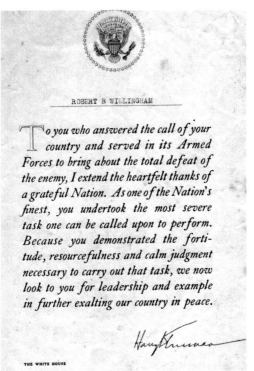

ROBERT B WILLINGHAM

To you who answered the call of your country and served in its Armed Forces to bring about the total defeat of the enemy, I extend the heartfelt thanks of a grateful Nation. As one of the Nation's finest, you undertook the most severe task one can be called upon to perform. Because you demonstrated the fortitude, resourcefulness and calm judgment necessary to carry out that task, we now look to you for leadership and example in further exalting our country in peace.

THE WHITE HOUSE

Letter of Commendation from President Truman

Neither can Willingham be called a publicity seeker. Quite the opposite, he has until now tried to keep his UFO story as low profile as possible, shying away from publicity that might have brought him additional "consequences." When filing his NICAP affidavit in 1978, he held back many details, and he requested that Todd Zechel use his middle name, Burton, instead of his given name. Later, when he provided more information to Zechel, seemingly Zechel never published it. Since then, Willingham has turned down most requests for interviews. "A lot of people have called me over the years, but I've told most of them that I'm not interested in talking. I've had a lot of problems with my legs and have been in a lot of pain for a long time. So, I've backed off from talking to people."

United States
Congressional Advisory Board

On behalf of the 232 Republican and Democratic Senators and Representatives in the Coalition for Peace Through Strength Caucus we hereby invite

Colonel Robert B. Willingham

to become an advisor and to serve on our United States Congressional Advisory Board.

CONGRESSIONAL CO—CHAIRMEN

Senator Jake Garn
Senator J. Bennett Johnston
Representative Jack F. Kemp
Representative Bill Chappell, Jr.

AMERICAN SECURITY COUNCIL
30TH ANNIVERSARY
SPECIAL RECOGNITION CERTIFICATE

To commemorate your dedication to the goals of a strong national defense and peace through strength:

Colonel Robert B. Willingham

During a July 2007 visit to Willingham's North Texas home, he proudly displayed to the authors a number of documents and photographs that he holds near and dear to his heart. These documents demonstrate what an important and distinguished military career Willingham had. Speaking to his credibility are letters of commendation for his military service, including one from President Harry S. Truman.

He also told us of his years of service as a Congressional advisor on military matters and as an intelligence operative for the American Security Council.

Despite his years of dedicated work for his nation, Willingham has been fighting the denial of his pension ever since the 1970s. His efforts received a major setback in 1973 when fire destroyed many of the nation's Army and Air Force personnel records, including Willingham's. "They told me that my records were destroyed in a fire and that they don't have enough information to reconsider my request. Every time I have any dealings with them, I have to show them the records that I have.

1973 Fire at National Personnel Records Ctr. In St. Louis (National Archives Photo)

He admits that he was hesitant to speak very much about the UFO incident after the initial pension denial. But lately, he does not care anymore. "Now I'm 82 years old. If I want to talk about it, I'll talk about it."

Still, the slamming of the security lid on Willingham's UFO encounter has done its work. The truth has been silenced for all these years. Realizing now that his remaining time is short, Willingham hopes that the complete disclosure contained in this book will finally help clear up the mystery and uncertainty that has plagued his life for so long.

13

OPERATION BLUE FLY

When Robert Willingham arrived at the UFO crash site near Langtry, Texas, he found a group of Mexican soldiers already onsite, guarding the wreckage. The Mexicans had established a secure perimeter around the crashed object, which appeared to be a silver-colored disc that was partially buried in a sandy mound, just south of the Rio Grande River. Willingham was struck by the fact that the Mexicans were making no effort to retrieve any of the crash debris. When he enquired about this, he was told by one of the soldiers that their orders were to secure the site until the "American air force" arrived to take control of the situation.

Forced at gunpoint to leave the scene of the crash, Willingham returned two weeks later, and, to his amazement, there was absolutely no remaining trace whatsoever of the crashed UFO he had seen with his own eyes. Obviously, the debris had been hauled away, and a careful "cleanup" of the area had been conducted to remove any residual evidence. This type of military "crash retrieval" operation has been noted in every major UFO crash incident since the 1940s.

By the time of Willingham's UFO encounter, the U.S. military had an established track record of investigating UFOs and suspected UFO crash sites. To fully understand how the Langtry crash incident was handled, we need to look at the remarkable story of how the military first became involved in investigating UFOs.

The U.S. military first became interested in learning more about UFOs in the early 1940s. General Douglas MacArthur, who at that time was commander of Allied Forces in the Southwest Pacific, was alarmed at the high number of UFO sightings by American pilots early in World War II.

Willingham, Early 1960s

Later in his life, General MacArthur was credited with making references to extraterrestrials on at least two public occasions, indicating that his interest in the subject was quite real. In October 1955, after a meeting with MacArthur in New York, Achille Lauro, the Mayor of Naples, Italy, told reporters, "He believes that because of the developments of science, all countries on earth will have to unite to survive and to make a common front against attack from other planets. The politics of the future will be cosmic, or interplanetary, in General MacArthur's opinion."

"MacArthur Fears Space War" was the next day's headline in the *Chicago Tribune*. Skeptics say that MacArthur's comments were taken out of context and sensationalized by unscrupulous journalists. However, the statement remains of high interest to UFO researchers in light of the general's reported involvement in UFO investigations of the early and middle 1940s.

General Douglas MacArthur, Circa 1943 (U.S. Army Photo)

MacArthur made an even more intriguing comment about extraterrestrials in a public address made on May 12, 1962 at the U.S. Military Academy. Although he was 84 at the time, clearly MacArthur was still fascinated by the idea of earth being contacted by extraterrestrial civilizations. "We deal now, not with things of this world alone, but with the illimitable distances and as yet unfathomed mysteries of the universe. We are reaching out for a new and boundless frontier. We speak in strange terms of harnessing the cosmic energy ... of ultimate conflict between a united human race and the sinister forces of some other planetary galaxy."

Perhaps MacArthur's public statements reveal why, back in the early 1940s, he seemed to be so interested in the subject of UFOs. It is certain that the general took notice of a February 25, 1942 incident in which the skies over Los Angeles, California, lit up with a massive display of unidentified flying objects and anti-aircraft fire. The U.S. Army expended 1,430 rounds of artillery in one hour trying to shoot down the mysterious objects and evidently did not hit a single thing.

The matter was of such grave concern to American military leaders that on the day after the event, General George Marshall, the U.S. Army's Chief of Staff, drafted a secret memorandum to President Franklin D. Roosevelt attempting to explain what happened. The text of the memo, which was declassified in 1974 under the Freedom of Information Act, follows:

SECRET
February 26, 1942.
OCS 21347-86

MEMORANDUM FOR THE PRESIDENT:

The following is the information we have from GHQ at this moment regarding the air alarm over Los Angeles of yesterday morning:

"From details available at this hour:

1. Unidentified airplanes, other then American Army or Navy planes, were probably over Los Angeles, and were fired on by elements of the 37th CA Brigade (AA) between 3:12 and 4:15 AM. These units expended 1430 rounds of ammunition.

2. As many as fifteen airplanes may have been involved, flying at various speeds from what is officially reported as being very slow to as much as 200 MPH and at elevations from 9000 to 18000 feet.

3. No bombs were dropped.

4. No casualties among our troops.

5. No planes were shot down.

6. No American Army or Navy planes were in action.

Investigation continuing. It seems reasonable to conclude that if unidentified airplanes were involved they may have been from commercial sources, operated by enemy agents for purposes of spreading alarm, disclosing location of antiaircraft positions, and slowing production through blackout. Such conclusion is supported by varying speed of operation and the fact that no bombs were dropped.

Gen. George C. Marshall
Chief Of Staff

Following this incident and the many sightings of "foo fighters" by U.S. pilots from 1943-1945 (*according to the Robertson Panel Report, 1953*), MacArthur may have participated in the formation of a top-secret Army UFO research group called the Interplanetary Phenomena Research Unit (IPU), in which General George C. Marshall was also involved. The IPU was the forerunner of Operation Blue Fly and Project Moon Dust, both of which were U.S. military efforts to recover "unidentified objects" that had entered the earth's atmosphere and crashed somewhere on the planet.

The IPU's existence has been confirmed in recent years, but no documents about it have ever been officially released. A military spokesman in 1984 stated that "... the so-called Interplanetary Phenomenon Unit (IPU) was disestablished and, as far as we are aware, all records, if any, were transferred to the Air Force in the late 1950s. The 'unit' was formed as an in-house project purely as an interest item for the Assistant Chief of Staff for Intelligence. It was never a 'unit' in the military sense, nor was it ever formally organized or reportable, it had no investigative function, mission or authority, and may not even have had any formal records at all. It is only through institutional memory that any recollection exists of this unit."

George C. Marshall (U.S. National Archives)

British UFO researcher Timothy Good, in 1987, received a similar response about the IPU: "...the aforementioned Army unit was disestablished during the late 1950s and never reactivated. All records pertaining to this unit were surrendered to the U.S. Air Force Office of Special Investigations in conjunction with operation Blue Book."

UFO researchers suggest that the Interplanetary Phenomenon Unit spawned the most mysterious and elite military UFO investigations group of the 1950s, called Operation Blue Fly. Operation Blue Fly is said to have been the U.S. military's first major attempt to establish top-secret, quick-response teams whose purpose was to secure areas where an unidentified flying object has crashed, to recover all artifacts and bodies left behind from the crash, and to cover up any remaining traces of the event. Only in recent years has more information come to light about these clandestine recovery teams and their operations.

In a 2002 article, Leslie Kean expands on the connection between Blue Fly and Bluebook, "In 1953, the Air Defense Command created the 4602nd Air Intelligence Service Squadron (AISS) and assigned it to the official investigations of UFOs. The squadron was headquartered at Ent Air Force Base, CO and soon moved to Fort Belvoir, VA with field units throughout the country. All UFO reports were to go through the 4602nd AISS prior to any transmission to Project Blue Book, a public relations project with no access to reports above the Secret level. The 4602nd AISS dealt with more sensitive cases of national security concern requiring a higher classification. Thus, many UFO reports bypassed Blue Book altogether."

Originally, Blue Fly's principal mission was to recover crashed aircraft, missiles, and, later, satellites that were of non-U.S. origin. What was not publicly known, many UFO researchers claim, is that Blue Fly operations also included the recovery of unidentified flying objects – objects that did not correlate with any known technology of the Soviet Union or any other nation on earth.

On August 12 1954, the Air Force released Regulation 200-2, titled "Unidentified Flying Objects Reporting (Short Title: UFOB)," which describes the 4602nd Air Intelligence Service Squadron as "composed of specialists trained for field collection and investigation of matters of air intelligence interest.... This squadron is highly mobile and deployed throughout the ZI [Zone of Interior]..." In this regulation is the unmistakable footprint of a top-secret rapid-deploy crash retrieval team reporting to the USAF Air Defense Command. The document speaks of highly-trained "specialists" who are specifically assigned to be ever at the ready to participate in the recovery of material that has crashed to Earth upon entry through our atmosphere.

6. ZI Collection. The Air Defense Command has a direct interest in the facts pertaining to UFOB's reported within the ZI and has, in the 4602d Air Intelligence Service Squadron (AISS), the capability to investigate these reports. The 4602d AISS is composed of specialists trained for field collection and investigation of matters of air intelligence interest which occur within the ZI. This squadron is highly mobile and deployed throughout the ZI as follows: Flights are attached to air defense divisions, detachments are attached to each of the defense forces, and the squadron headquarters is located at Peterson Field, Colorado, adjacent to Headquarters, Air Defense Command.

Excerpt from Air Force Regulation 200-2. August 1954

It is clear from a careful reading of this regulation that the Air Force in 1954 was concerned with securing and recovering any physical debris which might be found at the crash site of unknown aircraft. It outlines a policy that any materials resulting from a UFO encounter should be immediately safeguarded and kept for future analysis.

b. *Materiel.* Suspected or actual items of materiel which come into possession of any Air Force echelon will be safeguarded in such manner as to prevent any defacing or alteration which might reduce its value for intelligence examination and analysis.

Excerpt from Air Force Regulation 200-2. August 1954

The policy of having a super secret government group to deal with UFO phenomena continues to this day, according to many modern day UFO investigators. This secret group, hidden deep within the U.S. government's black operations budget, remains at constant readiness to recover unidentified objects that have fallen out of the sky.

Evidence seems to confirm that the U.S. military has had a strong interest in recovering crashed UFOs. In recent years, through the Freedom of Information Act, over 1,000 pages of previously classified government documents have been released that make reference to either Operation Blue Fly or Project Moon Dust, and, interestingly, a number of these references appear within the context of UFO incidents.

3. (U) TITLE: MOON DUST - OBJECT FOUND NEAR SANTA CRUZ.

16. SUMMARY: A REPORT HAS BEEN RECEIVED WITHIN THE EMBASSY AND REPORTED IN THE SANTA CRUZ NEWSPAPER OF AN UNIDENTIFIED OBJECT HAVING BEEN FOUND ON A FARM NEAR SANTA CRUZ.

ITEM 22. A. ON LATE AFTERNOON OF 790816 THE EMBASSY HERE RECEIVED INFORMATION THAT A STRANGE OBJECT HAD BEEN FOUND ON A FARM NEAR SANTA CRUZ, BOLIVIA. SOURCE STATED THAT THE OBJECT WAS ABOUT 70 CENTIMETERS

Project Moondust Reference (USAF FOIA)

Another document from the USAF Air Intelligence Agency, references Project Moon Dust within the context of a reported UFO crash near Santa Cruz, Bolivia. To veteran UFO researcher Ryan S. Wood, this document "provides additional intriguing details and references to Moon Dust, the prominent governmental space debris and UFO retrieval program designed to locate, recover, and deliver descended foreign space vehicles back to

Wright Patterson Foreign Technology Division headquarters for analysis and exploitation."

Other stories have surfaced recently from persons claiming to have been part of military crash retrieval operations, such as the startling tale told by an anonymous informant to longtime UFO researcher Elaine Douglass. Some years ago, Douglass made contact with a former soldier who claimed to have been on a military crash recovery team. "While I was MUFON state director Washington DC, I was contacted by an individual recently discharged from the military who told me something of interest indirectly related to the Mexican disc crash."

Elaine Douglass, UFO Researcher

"The individual told me that while he was in the military, he served with a unit whose function was to go inside foreign countries, perform some task and get out quickly without the government of the foreign country knowing the unit had been there."

Douglass says that she met with her informant, a man in his late thirties, in a Washington D.C. coffee shop, "He showed me his military records, which were in plastic sleeves in a 3-ring binder. He said that the unit he served with was stationed in the United States and was not unique. That is, that there are several such teams in readiness at all times."

Douglass remembers her informant saying that the rapid-deploy missions he had been involved in were always extremely high stress, and that it took the team members a long time after completion of their object to "unwind" and return to normalcy. According to the source, soldiers returning from these stealth missions were tense to the point of irrationality for a long period afterward. Anyone who irritated one of these men was in serious danger of being "punched out" by them.

According to Douglass, the informant did not describe in great detail any specific missions his rapid-deploy teams had performed. Also, he did not state that he himself had been involved in any UFO crash recoveries. However, he did indicate that recovering crashed UFO artifacts would have been well within the scope of the types of missions these groups undertook and had in fact undertaken in the past. "I recall him saying that he and his fellow servicemen used to stay up late at night talking about UFOs and extraterrestrials and wondering what was their ultimate significance," Douglass explains.

The team that recovered the Langtry UFO materials is exactly the type of unit that Douglass' anonymous ex-military informant was talking about. The quick incursion into Mexico, the recovery of the disc, and the removal of all evidence were the very kinds of missions described to Douglass by the man she met in Washington, D.C.

It seems clear that a crash recovery team, as described by Douglass' informant, arrived at the Langtry, Texas UFO crash site, shortly after Robert Willingham was forced to leave by the Mexican military. It is presumed that Blue Fly / Moon Dust operatives quickly arranged transport of the crashed disc and metallic debris, most likely by truck convoy across West Texas. Moving the object across the Rio Grande River was no problem, because as Willingham remembers, "the river was so shallow, that you could wade across it." The retrieval team then remained on the scene to ensure that not a single shred of evidence remained behind for any curious civilians who might have seen or heard the crash.

Sketch of UFO Recovery (Japan TV)

14

ALIEN BODIES

Shortly after his UFO encounter, Robert Willingham began hearing rumors that the bodies of at least two alien beings might have been recovered from the UFO crash site at some point after he visited the area. He was uncertain if the U.S. or Mexico had made the alleged recovery. "I kept hearing about bodies," Willingham remembers. "But I didn't know anything about it at that point."

1978 Japanese TV Artist's Sketch of Alleged Alien Bodies

Through a remarkable coincidence, Willingham later had a chance to talk about alien bodies with one of the Mexican soldiers whom he had met at the UFO crash site. When Willingham had originally gone to the crash site, he encountered an English-speaking Mexican army officer who identified himself as Lieutenant Martinez. Amazingly, six weeks later, Willingham came face to face with Martinez again during a short trip to Mexico City on behalf of the U.S. Air Force.

Willingham and several other Texas-based pilots delivered fifteen airplanes to the Mexican government approximately six weeks after Willingham's UFO encounter. After making the delivery of the aircraft, Willingham and six other pilots remained in Mexico City briefly, awaiting a return trip to Texas in a U.S. Air Force Douglas C-54. During this short layover, Willingham ran into the very Mexican officer whom he had spotted at the UFO crash site along the Texas-Mexico border.

As he moved over to talk to Lieutenant Martinez, Willingham thought back to the rumors he had heard about alien bodies having been recovered at the UFO crash site. Since these rumors were fresh on his mind, he remembers saying something like, "I heard there were some bodies found out there at that crash on the border."

"Not that I know of," Martinez replied.

"So, you didn't see any bodies when you were down there?" Willingham asked.

"No," answered Martinez.

When Willingham's UFO crash story began receiving some attention from UFO researchers in 1978, some people no doubt associated his case with stories of alien bodies being recovered at other reported UFO crash sites in Mexico. "I never saw bodies," Willingham reiterates, "I was not able to get close enough, and I don't know what happened after I left."

The events as related by Willingham would lead one to believe that, if bodies were present in the crashed UFO, they were removed not by the Mexican military, but by the U.S. recovery team. This conclusion is based on the words and actions of the Mexican soldiers who were guarding the wreckage when Willingham and Perkins arrived.

The Mexicans said that their orders were to guard the crash site until the "American air force" arrived. They were making no effort to collect or inspect any of the crash debris. For the most part, they were staying away from the UFO wreckage. Willingham noted that they seemed to have no interest in probing the wreckage or preparing it for transport.

Willingham also observed that the top section of the crashed UFO, to which he refers as the "dome," had separated during impact and was still virtually intact in the desert soil near the rest of the debris. Assuming that the beings who were piloting the ship had not escaped prior to the arrival of the Mexicans, their bodies would have most likely been found inside the dome by the U.S. recovery team when it arrived later, after Willingham and Perkins had left the scene.

```
    ***************
    * TOP SECRET *
    ***************
EYES ONLY TOP SECRET / MAJIC          T52-EXEMPT (E)
          EYES ONLY

On 07 July, 1947, a secret operation was begun to assure
recovery of the wreckage of this object for scientific study.
During the course of this operation, aerial reconnaissance
discovered that four small human-like beings had apparently
ejected from the craft at some point before it exploded.
These had fallen to earth about two miles east of the wreckage
site. All four were dead and badly decomposed due to action
by predators and exposure to the elements during the approx-
imately one week time period which had elapsed before their
discovery. A special scientific team took charge of removing
```

Excerpts from Eisenhower Briefing Document

If bodies of the UFO entities *were* recovered, how would they have been handled and processed by the U.S. military? For years, rumors have abounded that the government has secret facilities where these entities, both living and deceased, have been kept for study. When an alleged top-secret government document about UFOs surfaced in 1984, suddenly there seemed to be tangible evidence of the government's past involvement in retrieving UFO entities. The document, allegedly prepared for President Dwight Eisenhower, was dated November 18, 1952 and contained information about two UFO crashes – the famous one near Roswell, New Mexico, in 1947, and another one near Del Rio, Texas.

With reference to the Roswell crash, the document states, "On 07 July, 1947, a secret operation was begun to assure recovery of the wreckage of this object for scientific study. During the course of this operation, aerial reconnaissance discovered that four small human-like beings had apparently ejected from the craft at some point before it exploded. These had fallen to earth about two miles east of the wreckage site. All four were dead and badly decomposed due to action by predators and exposure to the elements during the approximately one week time period which had elapsed before their discovery. A special scientific team took charge of removing these bodies for study."

The document goes on to describe a scientific analysis of the four dead UFO entities conducted by Dr. Detlev Bronk. "It was the tentative conclusion of this group (30 November, 1947) that although these creatures are human-like in appearance, the biological and evolutionary processes responsible for their development has apparently been quite different from those observed or postulated in homo-sapiens. Dr Bronk's team has suggested the term 'Extra-terrestrial Biological Entities', or 'EBEs,' be adopted as the standard term of reference for these creatures until such time as a more definitive designation can be agreed upon."

Dr. Detlev Bronk – Conducted Alien Autopsies?

Although the document does not specifically mention the recovery of UFO entities from crash sites other than Roswell, one supposes that the military procedures would be similar. The location or locations where these recovered entities are kept surely represents one of the most-tightly controlled secrets in the history of our race.

Veteran researcher Stanton T. Friedman, in his book *Top Secret / Magic*, observes, "This preliminary briefing for Eisenhower notes that the characteristics of the humanlike bodies were different from those of *homo sapiens*." For additional clues about how the U.S. government might deal with UFO entities, Friedman points to another supposedly top-secret document discovered in 1984 titled *Extraterrestrial Entities and Technology, Recovery and Disposal*. The document outlines government procedures for the recovery of crashed space objects and any occupants thereof.

It makes sense that the government would have such a manual to be used by military personnel involved in the retrieval of objects reentering the earth from outer space. Friedman writes, "Various government agencies have had special retrieval teams whose activities and identification have been kept very low profile for decades.... Vehicles do crash. Highly classified, and sometimes highly radioactive, portions of satellites sometimes survive reentry into the atmosphere. Most of the members of rapid response have other jobs, but are ready to go at a moment's notice."

Friedman gives as an example the crash of a highly classified Stealth aircraft near Bakersfield, California – prior to the military confirming that the Stealth existed. "Security teams were in place very quickly, keeping people away from the crash site. They were followed by collection, packaging, and clean-up teams. These groups made sure that all the wreckage was recovered and that the ground was treated so that no one would be able to recover a piece of the high-technology skin of the vehicle. Civilians unfortunate enough to be caught up in the security web were made to sign silence agreements ending with the phrase *upon penalty of death* according to a witness who very quietly spoke to me about it after a lecture."

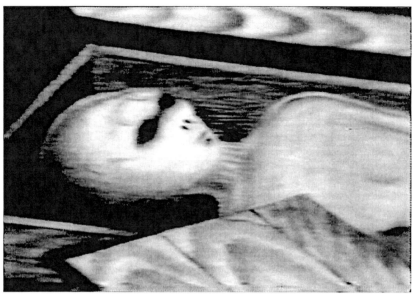

1978 Japanese TV Artist's Sketch of Alleged Alien Body

If the U.S. military did recover bodies from the UFO crash site visited by Willingham, it is obvious that the entities were whisked away very quickly and taken to a secret government research facility. "I sure would have liked to have seen them," Willingham says wistfully. "That's something I would really have liked to see."

15

WILLINGHAM, UFO HUNTER

Ironically, the Air Force reservist involved in one of the most compelling UFO cases of the 1950s was himself destined to become an investigator of UFOs for the Air Force's *Project Blue Book* in the early 1960s. During four years with *Blue Book* (circa 1959-1963), Colonel Robert Willingham assisted other investigators in taking over 2,000 witness testimonies from persons claiming to have had UFO encounters. Although he mostly helped with cases in Pennsylvania, New Jersey, and New York, Willingham occasionally went as far as Venezuela and Chile to participate in UFO investigations for the U.S. Air Force.

Badge Used by USAF OSI Agents

At the time, Willingham lived in Harrisburg, Pennsylvania, and worked as a metallurgist for the Laurel Pipeline Company. "We laid a pipeline from Philadelphia to Cleveland, Ohio, to deliver fuel, such as gasoline, jet fuel, heating oil – refined products. I worked for them for about ten years." It was during this time that *Blue Book* called, requesting the services of Air Force reservists in Harrisburg, including Willingham, to assist with UFO investigations.

Harrisburg was a headquarters (District 3) for the U.S. Air Force's Office of Special Investigations (OSI), and many *Blue Book* reports emanated from there. From 1947 to 1969, *Blue Book* (known earlier as *Sign* and later *Grudge*) served as the "public face" of the U.S. government's efforts to systematically and "scientifically" investigate all domestic UFO sightings. While many argue that *Blue Book*'s real function was to disprove the existence of UFOs regardless of the evidence, the project has nonetheless yielded a wealth of UFO information that continues to be studied today. Clearly though, Blue Book was not the U.S. government's first or last involvement with UFO investigations. It is also obvious that many government UFO investigations conducted during the period 1947-1969 were omitted from *Blue Book*, including Willingham's own 1955 encounter with a crashed UFO.

In an enlightening article about *Project Blue Book* written for the Central Intelligence Agency in the late 1960s, former *Blue Book* director Hector J. Quintanilla noted that in 1953 the U.S. government received a clear mandate from a scientific advisory panel known as the *Robertson Panel*. The panel of scientists, obviously alarmed at the prospect that the American public's obsession with UFOs could weaken the U.S. Cold War defensive posture, recommended "that the national security agencies take immediate steps to strip the unidentified flying objects of the special status they have been given and the aura of mystery they have unfortunately acquired.

Therefore, in 1953 by Air Force Regulation 200-2, set the specific objectives for the remaining years of *Blue Book*'s existence:

(1) To determine if UFO phenomena present a threat to the security of the United States.

(2) To determine if UFO phenomena exhibit any technological advances which could be channeled into U.S. research and development.

(3) To explain or identify the stimuli which caused the observer to report a UFO.

CONFIDENTIAL

DEPARTMENT OF THE AIR FORCE
HEADQUARTERS UNITED STATES AIR FORCE
WASHINGTON

THE INSPECTOR GENERAL USAF
3D DISTRICT OFFICE OF SPECIAL INVESTIGATIONS
1612 S. Cameron Street, Harrisburg, Pa.
MAILING ADDRESS: POST OFFICE BOX 709

3DO 24-165   18 September 1956

SPOT INTELLIGENCE REPORT

SUBJECT: (Confidential)
Sighting of Unidentified Flying Object at
Cowans Gap Area, Pennsylvania, at approxi-
mately 110145Z, September 1956

Blue Book Report Handled by Harrisburg OSI Office

During the 22 years it existed, *Blue Book* "investigated" 12,618 sightings. Critics of *Blue Book* point out that very little in-depth investigation occurred in most of the cases and that the Air Force was too quick to assign conventional explanations to unexplainable events. Although the Air Force admits to only 701 (six percent) totally unsolved *Blue Book* cases, many civilian UFO researchers say that when unsubstantiated "explanations" are factored out, at least 25 percent of the sightings were never adequately explained.

STATUS REPORT

PROJECT BLUE BOOK - REPORT NO. 12

FORMERLY PROJECT GRUDGE

~~SECRET~~
UNCLASSIFIED

~~SECURITY~~
~~INFORMATION~~

PROJECT NO. 10073

30 SEPTEMBER 1953

AIR TECHNICAL INTELLIGENCE CENTER
WRIGHT-PATTERSON AIR FORCE BASE
OHIO

Project Blue Book Summary Report Cover, 1953

Operating with an incredibly small staff and hardly any budget, *Blue Book* was ill prepared to conduct any credible UFO investigative work. "Our *Project Blue Book* office at Wright-Patterson has a complement of only one officer, two sergeants, and one civilian stenographer," wrote former *Blue Book* director Quintanilla in the late 1960s. Thus, many have surmised that investigating UFOs carefully and without bias was never really *Blue Book*'s plan. Its real purpose was "to denounce the UFOs, dismiss the UFOs, debunk the UFOs and anybody who believes in them -- just come up with answers and get this UFO thing out of the newspapers," according to Robert Goldberg, author of *Enemies Within: The Culture of Conspiracy in Modern America.*

Robert Friend, *Blue Book* director from 1958 to 1963 (when Willingham served), admitted in a 2005 interview with ABC News that the underlying directive was to explain away the UFO "mystery" as quickly as possible. "What they wanted to try to do was, I think, to re-educate the public regarding UFOs, to take away the aura of mystery," he stated.

Blue Book Scientist J. Allen Hynek (U.S. Government Photo)

Blue Book's chief scientific investigator, Dr. J. Allen Hynek, spent his years with the project as the military's greatest spokesman against the reality of UFOs. After leaving *Blue Book*, though, Hynek became a UFO believer and dedicated the rest of his life to studying the phenomenon. Commenting on his years with *Blue Book*, Hynek once said that the UFO sightings he found most difficult to explain away were those reported by military pilots (like Robert Willingham), because these highly skilled individuals were trained by the Air Force itself.

"They could say civilian pilots might've been untrustworthy, but they could hardly say that of their own military pilots. And we got case after case from military pilots, which never hit the press," Hynek said.

In the early 1960s, Willingham himself went from being a UFO witness to being an investigator of UFO cases like his own.

"We'd receive a report that somebody saw something and we would go check it out. We'd talk to all of the neighbors and other witnesses. We would write all of that down and turn it in to the person in charge of that section of *Blue Book*. Some of the witnesses were even Air Force personnel."

"Of the 2,000 cases that my *Blue Book* team looked at, I would say that at least half of them were totally unexplained," Willingham says. "We (the investigators) were told these objects might be Russian or from some other country, but nobody really believed that. The Russians didn't have anything that could fly 2,000 miles per hour. We didn't buy that."

F-100 Super Sabre Jet (NASA Photo)

During this time, Willingham took part in a couple of "UFO hunts" conducted by the U.S. Air Force in South America at the request of authorities there. "We were contacted by people down in South America who had seen these objects flying around and were very scared." Willingham recalls. "So I went down there in an F-100, and we flew surveillance looking for the UFOs in the places where they had been seen. Some of these were night missions, flying up and down the coast, hoping to run into something. We would spread out, about three miles apart, fly right down the coast, and then turn around and head back."

"If something was sighted at night, one of the planes would be sent out, and another would take off shortly afterward to provide cover for the first plane. We were armed but were instructed to fire only when we faced danger to our own plane. If they were doing something to screw up our airplane, we could fire."

Interestingly, Willingham says that he was ordered to log his missions to South America as "test flights" for the F-100 aircraft. "That was our cover story," Willingham says. "That's how I logged them."

"They told us they wanted us to go down there [to South America] to check it out. So I went with my squadron from Harrisburg, Pennsylvania," He recalls. "I told the oil company [Laurel Pipeline] I worked for that I'd be gone for a couple of weeks, and I took off. It was out of the Air Force's 192nd Interceptor Squadron that we were assigned to at that time, I believe. Usually, three or four of us would take part in that."

"The local people had requested that the U.S. military go down there and investigate this, because these things had scared some of those people pretty bad."

> Venezuela has been the scene of so much UFO activity that as of 1963, according to a NICAP member who visited Caracas, the sight of huge glowing objects lighting up mountain tops around the city was no longer considered noteworthy.
>
> During the 1962 sightings around Buenos Aires, as well as in remote areas of the country, key cases were reported freely on television. Argentina's treatment of the UFO question provides an interesting contrast with the secretive policy of the U.S. Government.

Report on Venezuela UFOs in Blue Book

The *Blue Book* archives confirm that Venezuela and Chile were a hotbed of UFO activity in the early 1960s. *Blue Book* contains a clipping from a NICAP article, which states, "Venezuela has been the scene of so much UFO activity that as of 1963, according to a NICAP member who visited Caracas, the sight of huge glowing objects lighting up mountain tops around the city was no longer considered noteworthy.... During the 1962 sightings around Buenos Aires, as well as in remote areas of the country, key cases were reported freely on television. Argentina's treatment of the UFO question provides an interesting contrast with the secretive policy of the U.S. Government."

Formations of UFOs, about 16 objects in all, passing from east to west between 4:00 and 6:00 p.m. were witnessed by many people in the Parque del Este, Caracas, February 11, 1962. One witness, Sr. Emiro Ayesta, ran to the Humboldt Planetarium in the park where Sr. Carlos Pineda of the Planetarium staff witnessed one of the UFOs. Sr. Pineda described it as "a body giving off a brilliant light, moving at great altitude as if towards the moon."

Report on Venezuelan UFOs (Project Blue Book)

Although, during his four years of working with *Blue Book*, Willingham did not see a UFO himself, he talked to many individuals who claimed to have seen one. "Many of the stories were credible. Of course we talked to a lot of nuts – people who just wanted to get their name in the paper. For example, we talked to one guy who claimed he was taken aboard a UFO for two days, but it turned out that he had really spent those two days sleeping with a mistress and didn't want his wife to know where he had been."

These false UFO reports, according to Willingham, account for only half of the cases that he looked into during his *Blue Book* years. Asked if he and the other *Blue Book* investigators he worked with ever voiced their own opinions about UFOs to each other, he says, "We talked about it and looked at what was being said in the newspapers and magazines, but nobody really knew what they were. That's why they were unidentified."

Regarding UFO crashes and the recovery of bodies from UFOs, Willingham remembers one particular incident from the middle 1960s that occurred in North Texas, somewhere near Dallas. Three bodies were recovered from the wreckage of a downed UFO. Willingham desired to go the location and find out more about what happened, but the incident was quickly draped in a veil of deep military secrecy. "They shut that one up really tight," He recalls. "It was hushed up very quickly, and we didn't hear anything more about it."

A second UFO crash with bodies took place in Colorado earlier in the 1960s. Although he heard enough about the incident to pique his interest, the military once more moved in very quickly with a thick veil of secrecy. "That was very top secret," He says.

In 1963 or 1964, Willingham resigned from *Project Blue Book* due to health issues. No longer able to fly and having to undergo numerous medical treatments, he no longer felt able to continue the UFO investigations.

16

SECRET AIRCRAFT

Coincidentally, Robert Willingham recalls flying over the site of a crashed top-secret military aircraft in the area of Laughlin Air Force Base in Del Rio in 1957. "I flew over one [a military crash site] and they shot at me," he remembers. "I flew over it at about 2,500 feet in an F-86, and they shot at me. They didn't hit me, but they shot at me. I could see the puffs on the rifles."

Lockheed U-2A Reconnaissance Plane (U.S. Air Force Photo)

Willingham remembers that the USAF recovery team had the area around the crash site sealed off, and they were serious about keeping everyone away. Speaking quickly into his radio, Willingham said, "Hey, quit shooting at me. I'm on your side." A voice crackled on his speaker from a person who identified himself as an Air Force colonel, telling him, "You're in a red zone. Get the hell out of here. We're busy down here."

After that, he quickly left the area. He did not find out until later that he had accidentally stumbled upon the crash site of one of the most secret military aircraft of the 1950s, the Lockheed U-2 spy plane, which was developed at Area 51 in Groom Lake, Nevada, but was later tested at Del Rio's Laughlin AFB. When Willingham later found out about the U-2 program, he understood why he had been ordered out of the "red zone" with such urgency.

The urgent need to keep the U-2 testing away from the prying eyes of the Soviets actually led to the development, in 1955, of Groom Lake, Nevada, as a testing facility for top-secret U.S. military aircraft. Later referred to as Lockheed's Skunk Works and used for testing some of the most advanced aircraft ever designed, Groom Lake began its existence as the home of the U-2. The first U-2 test flight at Groom Lake took place in August of 1955.

In 1957, further testing of the U-2 was assigned to the 4080th Strategic Reconnaissance Wing based in Del Rio, Texas, and the first U-2 high-altitude, long-range reconnaissance aircraft arrived at Laughlin Air Force Base on June 11, 1957. The U-2 could fly 10-hour missions at exceptionally high altitudes at a top speed of 600 mph. Shortly after the U.S. Strategic Air Command introduced the highly classified U-2 planes to Laughlin AFB, the aircraft began flying high altitude reconnaissance missions over countries behind the Iron Curtain.

About the selection of Laughlin AFB as the home base for U-2s, Michael Dobbs of the *Washington Post* wrote, "In order to preserve the secrecy surrounding the plane, the Air Force insisted on seclusion. The U-2 squadron was stationed outside Del Rio, Tex., a small town on the Mexican border three hours' drive from San Antonio. The base was surrounded by arid scrub, cactus and sagebrush. The pilots, flight technicians and administrators formed a tight knit community, living side by side in brand-new housing. Junior personnel were assigned air-conditioned duplexes with washer, dryer and carport, all the accouterments of '50s consumer society."

U-2 planes from the 4080th Strategic Reconnaissance Wing were credited with obtaining the first pictures of the Soviet missile build-up in Cuba during October of 1962, resulting in the Cuban Missile Crisis. The single casualty of the Crisis was Major Rudolph Anderson, of Laughlin Air Force Base, whose U-2 was shot down over Cuba. In an incident known to the Del Rio airmen as "Black Saturday," Anderson's spy plane was rocked by an exploding surface-to-air missile. Several pieces of missile shrapnel sliced through the cockpit, piercing the back of his helmet and his body suit.

The U-2 was actually the second highly-classified military plane to be based at Laughlin. In the early 1950s, the Air Force brought to Del Rio another famous U.S. spy plane, the RB-57 high-altitude reconnaissance aircraft. Because of its large size, the RB-57 could be filled with a wide range of electronic information gathering equipment.

RB-57 Aircraft in 1953 (U.S. Air Force Photo)

The U-2 crash witnessed by Robert Willingham in 1957 was one of five such mishaps that occurred in or around Del Rio during that time. The first two crashes happened in a single day, on June 28, 1957. Air Force pilot Ford E. Lowcock was killed when his plane went down near the Del Rio airport. Later on the same day, pilot Leo Smith died when his U-2 crashed.

In the fall of 1957, pilot Perkins Nole survived the September 26 crash of his aircraft. Two months later, on November 28,

Ben A. Lacombe ejected from his U-2 after it malfunctioned, but his parachute was caught on the aircraft's speed brake, killing the pilot. The final Del Rio area U-2 crash occurred on August 6, 1958. After a successful mission, pilot Paul L. Haughland was bringing his plane in on final approach when it suddenly crashed, claiming his life.

What is significant about the U-2 accidents near Del Rio is that they demonstrate how well prepared the U.S. military was for an aircraft crash retrieval operation in Southwest Texas. In each of the U-2 cases, the area around the crash was immediately cordoned off to civilian traffic. Aircraft were not allowed to fly over. The aircraft and all associated debris was quickly retrieved and carted away. All traces of the airplane crash were then meticulously removed. Thus, the secret U.S. spy plane remained a secret.

At the time, the U.S. government's official cover story was that the U-2 was a high altitude weather research aircraft. The research aircraft was operated by 'weather reconnaissance' squadrons, according to the government. Even routine landings of the plane were shrouded in secrecy, according to a May 16, 1960 *Time* magazine article, which reported, "Whenever a U-2 landed, military police swarmed around it. Its pilots were civilians, and when an airman would nudge up close at the officers' club bar to swap plane lore, the U-2 pilot would smile and move along."

The *Time* article also tells of the time in 1959 when a U-2 with engine trouble glided to a landing at a small airstrip near Tokyo, Japan, in full view of a number of Japanese civilians. "Fifteen minutes later, a U.S. Navy helicopter arrived, disgorged a squad of Americans in civilian clothes. For the first time the pilot opened his canopy, called, 'I'm O.K.,' and climbed out. The Japanese noted that he carried a pistol at his waist, that his flight suit bore no markings. Moments later more U.S. civilians arrived, drew pistols and ordered the Japanese away from the plane."

THE U-2 COVER STORY

In February 1956, while the controversy over balloon flights was still raging and the U-2 was completing its final airworthiness tests, Richard Bissell and his staff began working on a cover story for overseas operations. It was important to have a plausible reason for deploying such an unusual looking plane, whose glider wings and odd landing gear were certain to arouse curiosity.

Excerpt from Recently Declassified CIA Memo
(CIA FOIA Web Site)

It seems likely that the tactics used by the military to keep its experimental aircraft hidden from the public have also been employed to retrieve and hide crashed UFOs, as in the Willingham case. Even more intriguing is the fact that the U.S. military in the 1950s was already working hard to develop an unconventional aircraft with the flight characteristics that had been observed in UFOs. This leads one to theorize that Willingham's UFO may have been a classified military aircraft with an even higher level of secrecy than the U-2.

Some researchers have suggested that perhaps what Willingham saw streaking across the sky that day was an experimental unconventional aircraft being tested by the U.S. Air Force, such as the recently declassified disc-shaped aircraft called "Project Silver Bug," which was under development in 1955 at Wright-Patterson Air Force Base near Dayton, Ohio. A technical report detailing the Silver Bug disc was released in 1998, following a Freedom of Information Act request made by a UFO researcher. Although the aircraft was certainly not the only "saucer-shaped" vehicle to be scrutinized by the U.S. military, it is one of the few whose existence has been acknowledged by the U.S. government. Silver Bug certainly seems to be one of the first attempts by the government to duplicate some of the flight characteristics of UFOs.

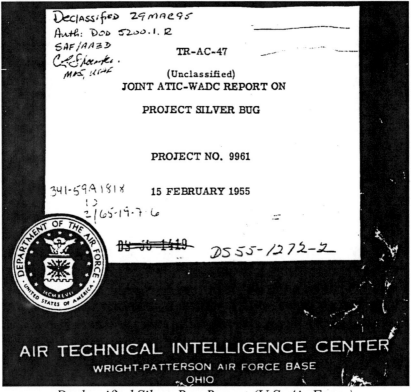

Declassified Silver Bug Report (U.S. Air Force)

Although the military has repeatedly denied that it has attempted to create aircraft based on the appearance and properties of UFOs, Project Silver Bug certainly tells a different story. As many scientists and engineers have pointed out, if UFO technology has been retrieved over the years by the U.S. government, it is most likely hundreds or thousands of years beyond what we are currently capable of manufacturing. We would not have access to the science, tools, and raw materials needed to begin to reproduce it. About the best that the military and its contractors could do in the 1950s is to try to apply some of the observed properties and characteristics of UFOs to unconventional aircraft already under development. It is highly unlikely that advanced UFO technology could be "reverse engineered" to a high degree;

however, studying it could provide government scientists with a "shortcut" in developing aircraft while remaining within the confines of conventional manufacturing technologies. Project Silver Bug certainly seems to fall within this theorized approach.

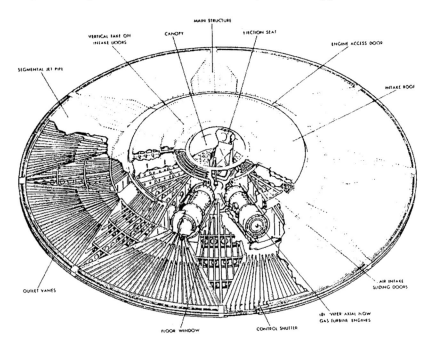

Fig. 2 Cut Away of Research Aircraft

Declassified Silver Bug Report (U.S. Air Force)

Clearly, the Silver Bug aircraft was a crude attempt by the Air Force to modify the aircraft technologies that existed in the 1950s and apply them to the creation of a vehicle capable of at least some of the flight characteristics of UFOs. Some researchers claim that the one-man aircraft, which was about 29 feet in diameter and about 4 feet tall, did actually fly and that it could attain an initial upward thrust of about 2,000 miles per hour. Officially, the military's position is that this vehicle never got past the theoretical stage, although perhaps other disc-shaped aircraft might have. Project Silver Bug was certainly not the only "flying saucer" type aircraft that has been on the U.S. military's drawing board over the years, although it is one of the few that has been declassified. According to researcher Richard Whitcomb, the U.S. at one point in the middle 1950s, "had as many as 35 saucer projects with vertical lift off and descent."

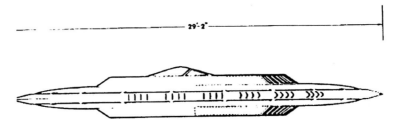

Fig. 3 Three-View General Arrangement of Research Aircraft

UNCLASSIFIED

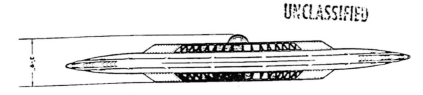

Declassified Silver Bug Report (U.S. Air Force)

Another recently declassified CIA document reveals that, during the late 1940s and early 1950s, the U.S. government took a great interest in the building UFO-type flying discs and feared that the Soviet Union already had such vehicles in their military arsenal. The CIA analysis, dated 1953, summarizes reports from several foreign newspapers which claimed that the Soviets might be flying German-made saucer-like aircraft in the skies over Africa, Iran, and Syria. George Klein, a German engineer, is quoted as saying that a "flying saucer" type aircraft was under development by Nazi Germany as early as 1941 and that Albert Speer, the Third Reich's Minister for Armament and Ammunition, personally attended the first experimental flight of the Nazi saucer on February 14, 1945 in Prague, Czechoslovakia.

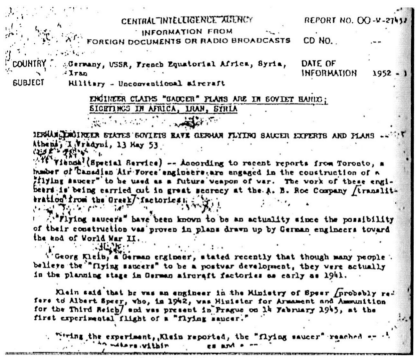

Declassified CIA Memo on Soviet UFOs

Another intriguing revelation in this CIA document is a top-secret effort by the Canadian Air Force to manufacture a "flying saucer to be used as a future weapon of war." Researcher Whitcomb states that the Canadian effort was backed by the U.S., which supplied a number of captured German scientists, including Dr. Richard Mehta, to assist with the development of a saucer craft. "These saucers were designed to fly 2,300 miles per hour at an altitude of 80,000 feet," Whitcomb writes.

The efforts of the Canadians eventually yielded a prototype craft called the Avrocar. Whitcomb writes, "The project, of which the Avro-Car was a part, was originally known as Project Y, funded by Canada, but was taken over by the U.S. Air Force in late 1953 - early 1954, as their Project 606, with an interest by the US Army. It was hoped that the vehicle, designated VZ-9V, would ascend vertically and reach flight speeds of 1,500 mph (2,400 km/hr). The President of Avro Canada wrote in *Aero News* that the prototype being built was so revolutionary that it would make other designs obsolete. The craft was officially named the Avro-Car. By 1960, about 10 million dollars had been spent on the project. During tests, the aircraft could not rise more than four or five feet above the ground without becoming very unstable. Attempts were made to design mechanisms to increase its stability without success. It was hoped that the project would consolidate the future of the A.V. Roe Company, but it was discontinued in 1961, and A.V. Roe went out of business... The Avro-Car was (depending on the source of the information) 18 or 25 feet in diameter, and weighed 3600 lb. It was powered by three centrally mounted gas turbine engines driving a 5 feet diameter central fan used for vertical takeoff. Once in the air the turbo-jet exhaust would be shifted to the rear giving the vehicle forward thrust to allow the aerodynamic body to generate lift."

Interestingly, Willingham recalls attending a demonstration of the Avrocar in 1958 or 1959 at Wright-Patterson Air Force Base in Ohio. "It didn't go up very far before beginning to wobble," Willingham remembers. "It was very unstable. I told the pilot that it didn't seem to me it would ever fly." Although he sat inside the Avrocar for a short time, Willingham politely declined an invitation to take the craft up for a test flight. "That thing was nothing like what I saw flying across the sky at 2,000 miles an hour," he adds.

While the Avrocar and the Project Silver Bug design seem relatively crude, rumors persist that the U.S. military has tested, and continues to test, much more sophisticated unconventional aircraft whose designs are based on UFOs. It is certainly possible that some of the disc-shaped aircraft seen by members of the public over the years may have been secret military flying vehicles.

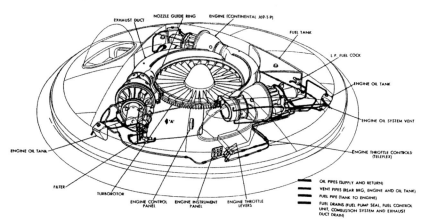

Avrocar (Courtesy Wikipedia.org)

How can one be certain that the crashed object Willingham saw near Langtry was not a top-secret military aircraft? "Someone could say that," Willingham responds, admitting that he was not able to closely inspect the crashed object for very long. "Might have been so, if it wasn't for that piece of metal. That piece of metal told me that it was something else, because I'm a pretty good metallurgist myself. It sure wasn't your common piece of metal. I've been welding since I was nine years old. My daddy was a blacksmith and a welder. I learned to acetylene weld when I was about nine or ten, and I worked with a lot of different metals."

Also hard to explain is the fact that the crashed object had earlier been seen traveling at over 2,000 miles per hour and executing a 90-degree turn while going at that incredibly high speed. None of the disc-shaped experimental aircraft projects declassified so far successfully attained these flight characteristics. Thus, Willingham remains firmly convinced that the object he saw crash along the Texas-Mexico border was "not anything that we or anybody else on earth made."

17

WHY UFOs CRASH

Robert Willingham does not know why the UFO he saw streaking across the skies of West Texas suddenly faltered in its flight and began heading down toward an eventual crash-landing several hundred feet south of the Rio Grande River. Before the object started descending, he observed that "there were a lot of sparks, and it tilted down by about a 45-degree angle." Since the disc first experienced problems after making a sharp 90-degree turn at over 2,000 miles per hour, Willingham wondered if the sudden turn might have caused something to fail inside the craft. But, he does not really know for sure.

Willingham UFO Crash Depicted in Sketch for Japanese TV

Willingham believes that after the object began having diffi-culty maintaining steady flight, it began to heat up. The rapidly intensifying heat caused the UFO occupants to attempt a crash landing in a body of water, perhaps even the shallow Rio Grande River, thus explaining why the UFO headed for the Texas-Mexico border. "These UFOs use some mechanism that makes them lighter than air. I don't know what it is, but it causes them to be lighter than air and allows them to go very fast and make very sharp turns. It seems to me if we [the U.S. military] have been able to study these things for so many years that we would have already figured out something about how they are able to do what they do."

If UFOs are, as some say, the highly sophisticated interstellar spacecraft of a technologically advanced civilization, why do they crash? The most commonly suggested explanations for UFO crashes are:

(1)   An internal failure of the UFO itself due to any num-ber of causes. If UFO occupants are mortal, they are fallible and thus subject to error.

(2)   Damage caused by conventional weaponry used by pursuing aircraft or ground based stations. As dis-cussed in this chapter, the U.S. military has, in the past, attempted to shoot down UFOs.

(3)   A failure of key UFO systems caused by intentional or unintentional electromagnetic interference gener-ated by human technologies, such as radar.

Robert Willingham could not completely rule out that the UFO he saw might have previously sustained damage resulting from U.S. military intervention. By the time he encountered it, the object had already zoomed across western Canada, triggering the Distant Early Warning radar system, and had moved across the western U.S. into Texas. Shortly after he saw it speed past him heading for the Mexican border, the airship began having trouble maintaining level flight. Could the U.S. military have fired at it along its route from Canada down to Texas?

In 1952, Americans were shocked to hear an admission by the Air Force that its pilots had standing orders to chase UFOs and shoot them down if they refused to land. This policy was reported widely in a series of newspaper and wire reports throughout the nation. "The Air Force revealed today that jet pilots have been placed on a 24 hour nation wide alert against 'flying saucers' with orders to 'shoot them down' if they refuse to land," reported the *Seattle Post-Intelligencer* on July 29, 1952. "It was learned that pilots have gone aloft on several occasions in an effort to shoot the mysterious objects to the ground but never came close enough to use their guns."

The Seattle newspaper also quoted an Air Force information officer, Lt. Col. Moncel Monte, as saying, "The jet pilots are, and have been, under orders to investigate unidentified objects and to shoot them down if they can't talk them down."

Air Force Orders Jet Pilots To Shoot Down Flying Saucers If They Refuse To Land

WASHINGTON July 28 (INS) - The Air Force revealed today that jet pilots have been placed on a 24 hour nation wide alert against "flying saucers" with orders to "shoot them down" if they refuse to land.

It was learned that pilots have gone aloft on several occasions in an effort to shoot the mysterious unidentified objects and to shoot them down if they can't talk them down.

In Air Force parlance, this means that if a "flying saucer" refuses to obey an order to land, jet pilots are authorized to shoot them to earth, if they can get close enough to do so.

...reference Tuesday on the celestial objects.

Capt. E. J. Ruppelt, a "flying saucer" specialist of the Air Technical Center in Dayton, left late Monday for Washington with a team of fellow officers.

Disclosure of the 24 hour alert came as new reports continued to pour into the Pentagon of...

Article from Seattle Post-Intelligencer, 7/29/1952

The disclosure about the Air Force's alert and shoot-down policy came in the wake of an unprecedented wave of UFO sightings throughout the country during the first half of 1952. The *Post-Intelligencer* noted that Air Force officials complained of being inundated by more than 100 new reports each month.

In a story titled, "Jets Told to Shoot Down Flying Discs," Darrell Garwood, a reporter for the International News Service (INS), stated, "Several pilots, according to the Air Force, have tried to shoot down the mysterious discs but the 'steady bright lights' in the sky have out flown the pilots by as much as a thousand miles an hour." Garwood's story, which was published in the July 29, 1952 edition of the Fall River (Massachusetts) *Herald-News*, also quotes Air Force officials as expressing frustration that their 600-mile-per-hour jet aircraft were unable to come within shooting range of the "blinking, enigmatic flying discs."

Alarmed by all the talk of UFOs being shot down, the president of the *United States Rocket Society*, Robert L. Farnsworth, sent an urgent telegram to President Harry Truman, Secretary of Defense Robert Lovett, and the secretaries of the Army and Navy, warning them not to fire upon UFOs. Farnsworth emphasized that hostile action might alienate mankind from "beings of far superior powers." Implicit in Farnsworth's warning is that these alien beings ought not to be trifled with or they might be provoked into shooting back.

Jets Told to Shoot Down Flying Discs

Air Force Puzzled But No Longer Skeptical

By DARRELL GARWOOD
WASHINGTON, (INS)—The Air Force, stumped by the inability of 600-mile-an-hour jet planes to catch "flying saucers," turned today to a new type camera to solve the 5-year-old sky mystery.

An AF spokesman said a new-type camera may be able to bring the mystery to an end. He said the camera photographs "luminous phenomenon." It uses the principle employed by astronomers in determining the composition of stars. Air Force scientists hope to determine the physical makeup of the source.

Maj. Gen. John A. Samford, chief of Air Force Intelligence, said the

The Air Force contended that its intensive investigation of more than 1,000 "saucer" reports has convinced it that they are not being sent over the United States by an enemy.

The AF added that its investigation indicated also that they are not being controlled by "a reasoning body."

Forty-eight hours of intensive investigation has failed to explain radar and visual observation of unidentified objects accompanied by brilliant white and colored lights

Article in Fall River (MA) Herald-News, 7/29/1952

"Would it be surprising if they decided to retaliate?" asks UFO researcher Stanton T. Friedman in a June 2005 column in the *MUFON UFO Journal*. Friedman notes that documentation exists of numerous cases from the early 1950s in which U.S. jet fighters chased UFOs in an apparent attempt to shoot them down. This is also a time period in U.S. history (beginning in the late 1940s) when an extraordinary number of military and civilian aircraft crashed, many under mysterious circumstances. Could the UFOs have been "shooting back"?

Another startling revelation about UFOs was published on July 29, 1952 in the celebrated *Washington Post* column *Washington Merry-Go-Round*, written by noted muckraking reporter Drew Pearson. "The Air Force, long skeptical about flying saucers, has now made some official and important admissions," Pearson wrote. "Admission No. 1 is that they have now detected something that looks like flying saucers on radar at the same time that people have claimed they saw flying saucers." To Pearson, this meant the discs were tangible and substantial, rather than optical illusions or hallucinations.

The Air Force's second admission, according to Pearson, was "that flying saucers could possibly be space ships from another planet." Pearson added that U.S. scientists in 1952 already had the basic designs to build an interplanetary spacecraft. "If we are this close to interplanetary travel, Air Force officers admit that a more advanced civilization could be keeping this planet under surveillance through flying saucers," he wrote.

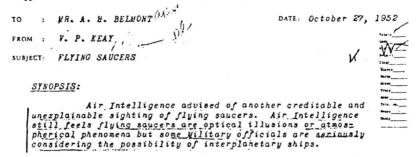

Memo about "Interplanetary Ships" (FBI FOAI Web Site)

Veteran UFO researcher Dr. Bruce Maccabee points out that in 1952 the Air Force informed the FBI that because so many UFO cases could not be explained, top Air Force personnel were seriously considering the interplanetary hypothesis. An FBI memo from October 27, 1952 states, "Air Intelligence advised of another creditable and unexplainable sighting of flying saucers. Air Intelligence still feels flying saucers are optical illusions or other atmospheric phenomena but some military officials are seriously considering the possibility of interplanetary ships. You will recall that Air Intelligence has previously kept the Bureau advised regarding developments pertaining to Air Intelligence research on the flying saucer problem."

L. Gordon Cooper Reported Several UFO Encounters
(NASA Photo)

U.S. astronaut L. Gordon Cooper, a jet fighter pilot in the 1950s, certainly agreed with the interplanetary hypothesis. "I believe that these extraterrestrial vehicles and their crews are visiting this planet from other planets," Gordon said in testimony given to the United Nations, "Most astronauts are reluctant to discuss UFOs.... I did occasion in 1951 to have two days of observation of many flights of them of different sizes, flying in fighter formation, generally from east to west over Europe."

Like Willingham, "Gordo" Cooper flew F-84 and F-86 jets from 1950 to 1954, mainly during his time with the 86th Fighter Bomber Group at Landstuhl, West Germany. He reported his first encounter with a UFO in 1951 and also had knowledge of numerous other sightings reported by pilots he knew and trusted.

"It was in Europe in 1961, that I saw my first UFO," Cooper wrote in his autobiography *Leap of Faith*. "When the alert sounded, my squadron mates and I dashed from the ready room and scrambled skyward in our F-86s to intercept the bogies. We reached our maximum ceiling of around forty-five thousand feet, and they were still way above us, and traveling much faster. I could see that they weren't balloons or MIGS or like any other aircraft I had seen before. They were metallic silver and saucer-shaped. We couldn't get close enough to form any idea of their size; they were just too high."

Cooper's startling account continued, "For the next two or three days, the saucers passed over the base daily. Sometimes they appeared in groups of four, other times as many as sixteen. They could outmaneuver and outflank us seemingly at will. They moved at varying speeds – sometimes very fast, sometimes slow – and other times, they would come to a *dead stop* as we zoomed past underneath them. We had no idea whether they were looking at us or what they were doing … If they weren't from anywhere here on Earth, we wondered aloud – *Where did they come from?*"

That certainly was the question on former U.S. Senator Barry Goldwater's mind when he too had a UFO encounter while piloting an F-86 jet in the skies over Arizona. Goldwater later told L. Gordon Cooper, "I chased it all over the desert and couldn't get near it. Damnedest thing I ever saw. Made me a believer."

With so many sightings of UFOs by military personnel, did the U.S. institute a policy in 1952 to track their movements? *Washington Post* columnist Drew wrote, "It has not been announced, but scientific observation posts have been set up in

New Mexico, where we are testing guided missiles, to track flying saucers also. A number of flying saucers have been seen in the Southwest, and since trained specialists are already on the job in that area with the latest scientific gadgets, the Air Force has ordered them to watch for flying saucers and track them scientifically."

Many were stunned by award-winning *Washington Post* journalist Drew Pearson's statement that the U.S. government had given specific orders for its scientists in New Mexico and "the Southwest" to "watch for flying saucers" and to track them using "the latest scientific gadgets." This eye-opening admission aligns with other reports of this time period about "experimental" radar stations established by the government in New Mexico to track and to possibly interfere with the guidance systems of the mysterious flying discs.

In Robert Willingham's account of the Langtry crash retrieval, he mentioned that the UFO was picked up by U.S. military radar as it streaked across the skies of the northwestern U.S., eventually slamming into the earth just south of the Rio Grande River near Del Rio. Similarly, in other reported UFO crashes of the late 1940s and early 1950s, the crashes were said to have occurred after the mysterious objects were tracked by military radar. Were the U.S. radar systems merely tracking the UFOs, or were their signals somehow interfering with the highly advanced guidance and navigation systems of these mysterious spacecraft?

Could the sudden introduction of experimental radar beams in the Southwestern United States in the late 1940s have somehow contributed to the many reports of crashed UFOs during this time period? Could the diminishing of UFO crash reports by the latter 1950s indicate that the UFO occupants adjusted their guidance and navigation systems to compensate for the presence of these and other electromagnetic signals present in the air over the United States?

DEW Radar Installation in Alaska, 1956 (Dept. of Defense Photo)

The concept that secret U.S. radar stations might have either intentionally or unintentionally caused some of the UFO crashes reported in the 1940s and 1950s remained an obscure notion held by a small group of UFOlogists until the year 1999. That's when the New Mexico state legislature designated as a National Historic Place a once-secret experimental microwave radar station at El Vado in Rio Arriba County, north of Los Alamos.

El Vado, whose construction in 1947 was personally authorized by U.S. President Harry S. Truman, functioned in secret from 1948 to 1958, and was known officially as Tierra Amarilla Air Force Station P-8. El Vado eventually became part of NORAD, the North American Air Space Defense Command.

The New Mexico Legislature's *House Joint Memorial 52*, introduced in 1999 by then State Representative J. "Andy" Kissner, states: "A joint memorial requesting the Northern New Mexico State School and the Office of Cultural Affairs to cooperate in nominating the El Vado radar site to the National Register of Historic Places and developing a management plan. Whereas, following World War II and the establishment of Los Alamos as a weapons research and development facility, the air force constructed a series of radar installations as part of a defense system around Los Alamos; and one of those facilities was located on a one hundred acre site near El Vado lake; and the site was abandoned and turned over to the state thirty years ago and is now owned by northern New Mexico state school; and ... the site represents one of the few cold war sites in northern New Mexico that is suitable for public interpretation...."

U.S. Radar Installation (NOAA Photo)

According to Kissner, the Tierra Amarilla station in El Vado (AFS-P8) was one of three secret radar installations in New Mexico during the late 1940s. The other two were Moriarty (AFS-P7) and Continental Divide (AFS-P51). Kissner says that the El Vado station was specifically assigned the task of helping to protect the Los Alamos Laboratory and the Atomic Energy Commission's atomic bomb production at Los Alamos and Sandia Base.

Kissner has stated that all three secret New Mexico radar sites hosted elements of the military's 4062nd AISS Group, which has been linked to Project Blue Fly, the top secret government unit charged with recovering crashed UFOs in the 1950s. In an interview with Linda Moulton Howe of *Earthfiles.com*, Kissner said that these secret radar installations were

established specifically to deal with the problem of the high
number of UFO sightings near sensitive U.S. military bases. "I
think this activity of these anomalous objects were definitely
something that interested the military from the standpoint of
where they were appearing and that the areas in which they were
appearing, especially in southern New Mexico, with the [atomic]
research related activity they had going on down there," Kissner
said.

Kissner added, "Any anomalous object that flew into this
area would have been considered, and not knowing what it is, I
think the assumption would have been that they were hostile.
And not knowing their source or anything about what these
things might represent. And because of our existing air defense
capability, I think it would be a natural assumption that we
would consider those things to be hostile and do something
about it."

C
9
P
I

CONFIDENTIAL

HEADQUARTERS FOURTH ARMY
Fort Sam Houston, Texas

/dcb

452.1 AKADB   13 January 1949

SUBJECT: Unconventional Aircraft (Control No. A-1917).

2. Agencies in New Mexico are greatly concerned over these phenomena. They are of the opinion that some foreign power is making
"sensing shots" with some super-stratosphere devise designed to be self-
disentergrating. They also believe that when the devise is perfected
for accuracy, the disentegrating factor will be eliminated in favor of
a warhead.

5. It is felt that these incidents are of such great importance,
especially as they are occurring in the vicinity of sensitive installations,
that a scientific board be sent to this locality to study the situation
with a view of arriving at a solution of this extraordinary phenomena with
the least practicable delay.

Excerpts from Memo about "Green Fireballs"

Veteran UFO researcher Bruce Maccabee points out that in
the late 1940s and early 1950s, the U.S. military grew highly
concerned about numerous sightings of unexplained "green fireballs" streaking across the skies over key military installations in

New Mexico and the Southwest. *Wikipedia* describes these phenomena as being "of notable concern to the U.S. government because they were often clustered around sensitive research and military installations, such as Los Alamos and Sandia National Laboratory; then Sandia base." Intense investigation determined that these objects were probably not meteors or flares, and they remain unexplained to this day. Apparently, the undeniable existence of these fireballs also led the government to take a more aggressive posture against UFOs.

J. "Andy" Kissner believes that these and similar incidents resulted in the U.S. military having a definite mandate to defend the air space above New Mexico. UFOs had to be assumed to be hostile, especially since they tended to appear over high-security U.S. military installations. Kissner also believes that there may be a tie-in between these secret radar sites and a rash of civilian and military aircraft crashes that occurred in 1947 and 1948. Kissner says, "During that period of time ... we had hundreds of airplane accidents in the United States. And that was all kinds of aircraft. And President Truman called a special board ... in early June 1947 to investigate the air crashes. There never was a final report." Howe and Kissner have suggested that the U.S. military had a policy in the 1940s and 1950s of shooting down UFOs with an experimental beam of some kind, but the practice was terminated after the UFOs began "shooting back" and causing the crash of numerous U.S. aircraft.

What about today? Does the U.S. military still keep a wary eye toward the heavens, while continuing to experiment with means of defending the Earth against UFOs? Is it possible that the U.S. government is preparing itself not just for hostile actions by other nations but also for possible attacks by extraterrestrial beings? Could U.S. dabblings into "Star Wars" type weaponry, such as the Starfire experimental laser testing program started in the 1990s, be the latest form of a strategy dating back to the 1940s designed to protect earth from the ever-present unidentified flying objects and their unearthly occupants?

Targeting UFOs may not be such a good idea, according to longtime researcher Ruben Uriarte. "The military can target a UFO, but shooting down these craft may present hostile consequences." To illustrate this point, researcher Bruce Maccabee cites the hostile encounter in 1976 between a UFO and two Iranian F-4 fighter jets in the skies over Tehran, Iran. The first jet approached the mysterious object, but lost instrumentation and communications. After it returned to base, a second F-4 arrived on the scene, and it experienced electromagnetic interference to its instruments. The second jet experienced a weapons systems failure when the pilot attempted to fire missiles at a smaller object that had broken off from the main UFO. "Basically, the UFO disabled the jet's weapon systems," Maccabee says.

As the F-4 continued pursuit south of Tehran, a second brightly-lit object (about one-half to one-third the size of the moon) detached from the original UFO and headed straight for the F-4 at a high rate of speed. The pilot attempted to fire an AIM-9 missile at the new object but was prevented by a sudden power loss in his weapons control panel. UHF and internal communications were simultaneously lost. The pilot promptly initiated a turn and negative-G dive to escape, but the object fell in behind the F-4 at 3-4 NM distance. Continuing the turn, the pilot observed the second object turn inside of him and then away, subsequently returning to the primary UFO for a perfect rendezvous.

U.S. Intelligence Report On Iranian UFO Incident

Perhaps the most famous case in which UFOs were believed to have disabled weapon systems was the 1967 Malstrom AFB incident in central Montana. Several aboveground observers spotted one or more UFOs hovering in the sky over underground nuclear missile silos. Shortly thereafter, ten nuclear-tipped Minutemen strategic missiles, alarmingly, began shutting down, one at a time.

The missile shutdowns were not caused by a loss of electrical power. Rather, the missiles experienced a disruption of their guidance and control systems, possibly from a targeted burst of electromagnetic pulse (EMP) energy. If, as many researchers believe, the missiles were deactivated by one or more UFOs hovering overhead, the attack was carefully aimed to knock out only the missiles.

The following is the investigation of Echo Flight incident

and the results. (U)

On 16 March 1967 at 0845, all sites in Echo (E) Flight,

Malmstrom AFB, shutdown with No-Go indication of Channels 9 and

12 on Voice Reporting Signal Assemble (VRSA). All LF's in E

Flight lost strategic alert nearly simultaneously. No other Wing

I configuration lost strategic alert at that time. 60

ACTION: OOAMA (OOCNCI/OOWE-COL DAVENPORT). INFO: 15AF
(DM4CI), 341SMW (DCM), BOEING AFFRO (D.J. DOWNEY, MINUTEMAN
ENGINEERING) BSD (BSS, SSQR)
SUBJECT: LOSS OF STRATEGIC ALERT, ECHO FLIGHT, MALSTROM
AFB. (U)
REF: MY SECRET MESSAGE DMTB 62751, 17 MAR 67, SAME SUBJECT.
ALL TEN MISSILES IN ECHO FLIGHT AT MALMSTROM LOST STRAT ALERT WITHIN
TEN SECONDS OF EACH OTHER. THIS INCIDENT OCCURRED AT 6845L ON
16 MARCH 67. AS OF THIS DATE, ASS MISSILES HAVE BEEN RETURNED TO STRAT

FOR OOAMA. THE FACT THAT NO APPARENT REASON FOR THE LOSS OF TEN
MISSILES CAN BE READILY IDENTIFIED IS CAUSE FOR GRAVE CONCERN TO THIS
HEADQUARTERS. WE MUST HAVE AN IN-DEPTH ANALYSIS TO DETERMINE CAUSE
AND CORRECTIVE ACTION AND WE MUST KNOW AS QUICKLY AS POSSIBLE WHAT
THE IMPACT IS TO THE FLEET, IF ANY. REQUEST YOUR RESPONSE BE IN KEEP-
ING WITH THE URGENCY OF THE PROBLEM. WE IN TURN WILL PROVIDE OUR
FULL COOPERATION AND SUPPORT.

Excerpts from Military Reports about Missile Shutdown

These cases suggest that UFOs are capable of disrupting human weapons and defense systems. There have even been cases of U.S. military aircraft being lost during UFO encounters. All of which emphasize the assertions of many researchers who suggest that aggressive military action against UFOs is not advisable.

18

MAJESTIC DOCUMENT

A brief account of Robert Willingham's UFO encounter was first made public in an isolated corner of the country in 1967. That was when he gave a general account of his encounter to a newspaper reporter in Mechanicsburg, Pennsylvania. Ten years passed before Todd Zechel picked up a clipping of the Pennsylvania story, tracked Willingham down, had him file an affidavit with NICAP, and began developing more information about the case. Some of the early information about the Willingham incident was distorted and inaccurate. Willingham himself contributed to some of the early confusion, as he was still suffering the lingering effects of a head injury sustained in Korea.

Until 1984, the only UFO crash retrieval associated with the region around Del Rio, Texas was based on Willingham's story of his encounter. Then, in 1984, some seventeen years after Willingham first spoke publicly about his case, a mysterious document appeared that discloses a UFO crash retrieval about 75 miles south of Del Rio said to have occurred on December 6, 1950, about five years before the Willingham case. This crash reportedly occurred along the Rio Grande River on the Mexican side, about halfway between El Indio, Texas and Guerrero, Coahuila, Mexico.

Rumors of the 1950 crash began when television documentary producer Jaime Shandera received from an anonymous source an undeveloped roll of film containing what appears to be a government document that mentions both the Roswell UFO crash of 1947 and a "second" crash near El Indio-Guerrero in 1950. Dated November 18, 1952, the *Eisenhower Briefing Document* (see Appendix) claims to have been authored by Rear Admiral Roscoe Hillenkoetter, the first CIA director, to brief incoming president Dwight Eisenhower on government-

148

sponsored UFO investigations. The document lists the members of a top-secret government committee on UFOs codenamed *Majestic-12* and discusses U.S. efforts to conceal the crashed alien spaceships retrieved from both Roswell and El Indio-Guerrero.

Willingham with Vintage Biplane, Early 1960s

The briefing document begins with a summary of the first recorded UFO sighting of the aviation era, "On 24 June, 1947, a civilian pilot, flying over the Cascade Mountains in the State of Washington observed nine flying disc-shaped aircraft traveling in formation at a high rate of speed." Many more sightings followed, the document states, and the U.S. military tried numerous different tactics for determining what these UFOs were and whether they posed a national threat. "In spite of these efforts, little of substance was learned about the objects until a local rancher reported that one had crashed in a remote region of New Mexico located approximately seventy-five miles northwest of Roswell Army Air Base (now Walker Field)."

In a staggering revelation, if true, the document describes the government's role in covering up the Roswell crash: "On 07 July, 1947, a secret operation was begun to assure recovery of the wreckage of this object for scientific study. During the course of this operation, aerial reconnaissance discovered that four small human-like beings had apparently ejected from the craft at some point before it exploded. These had fallen to earth about two miles east of the wreckage site. All four were dead and badly decomposed due to action by predators and exposure to the elements during the approximately one week time period which had elapsed before their discovery. A special scientific team took charge of removing these bodies for study. The wreckage of the craft was also removed to several different locations. Civilian and military witnesses in the area were debriefed, and news reporters were given the effective cover story that the object had been a misguided weather research balloon."

TOP SECRET / MAJIC

NATIONAL SECURITY INFORMATION

EYES ONLY

· · · · · · · · · · · · · ·
· TOP SECRET ·
· · · · · · · · · · · · · ·

EYES ONLY   COPY ONE OF ONE.

BRIEFING DOCUMENT: OPERATION MAJESTIC 12

PREPARED FOR PRESIDENT-ELECT DWIGHT D. EISENHOWER: (EYES ONLY)

18 NOVEMBER, 1952

Cover Page of the Eisenhower Briefing Document

After explaining that the military was continuing its research into the remains of the craft and its occupants, the Eisenhower

Briefing Document then suddenly mentions another crash similar in nature to Roswell: "On 06 December, 1950, a second object, probably of similar origin, impacted the earth at high speed in the El Indio - Guerrero area of the Texas - Mexican border after following a long trajectory through the atmosphere. By the time a search team arrived, what remained of the object had been almost totally incinerated. Such material as could be recovered was transported to the A.E.C. facility at Sandia, New Mexico, for study."

Shortly after the *Eisenhower Briefing Document* came to light, a leading UFO researcher, Kevin D. Randle, in his 1991 book *UFO Crash at Roswell*, called the El Indio-Guerrero incident "the second legitimate crash" after Roswell. "Although not as well documented as the Roswell case, there is good reason to believe that something extraordinary happened there," Randle wrote.

TOP SECRET / MAJIC
EYES ONLY

• TOP SECRET •

On 06 December, 1950, a second object, probably of similar origin, impacted the earth at high speed in the El Indio - Guerrero area of the Texas - Mexican boder after following a long trajectory through the atmosphere. By the time a search team arrived, what remained of the object had been almost totally incinerated. Such material as could be recovered was transported to the A.E.C. facility at Sandia, New Mexico, for study.

Excerpt from Eisenhower Briefing Document 11-18-52

The *Eisenhower Briefing Document* itself draws comparisons between the 1947 Roswell and El Indio-Guerrero crashes. It states that the latter crashed object was "probably of similar origin" to the Roswell UFO. The document also implies that the government used similar procedures for recovery of the alien artifacts in both cases.

In examining the account of the 1950 El Indio-Guerrero crash, there are numerous reasons why it clearly is not the same crash that Willingham witnessed. Let us examine how the two stories differ, and why they describe two different events:

Date

The *Eisenhower Briefing Document* states that the El Indio-Guerrero UFO crash occurred on December 6, 1950. Coincidentally, this was the date of a very famous "nationwide UFO alert" issued to the U.S. military, as we will explain in a later chapter. Robert Willingham, on the other hand, says his encounter occurred in 1955, although the exact date is unclear.

Willingham could not have been involved in the December 6, 1950 event, because he was serving in the Korean War at the time. He had been in Korea approximately four months when he was injured by a mortar shell on December 27, 1950.

Location

The *Eisenhower Briefing Document* states that the UFO crashed in a desolate area of Mexico, about 75 miles south of Del Rio, midway between El Indio, Texas and Guerrero, Coahuila. We have more to say about this location later. However, Willingham says the crash site he visited was in Langtry, Texas, more than 60 miles northwest of Del Rio. Although both locations can be said to be generally "near" Del Rio, neither place is truly Del Rio. El Indio and Guerrero are actually much closer to Eagle Pass, Texas, than they are to Del Rio. As in the Roswell incident, UFO cases are often associated with the nearest large city, as opposed to the exact location of the event.

In early statements about the incident, Willingham may have mentioned Laredo, which is 150 air miles from Del Rio, as a reference point, and journalists who were more familiar with Laredo than Del Rio used it as the crash location for Willingham's case. A distance of 150 miles may seem like a lot, but for someone traveling in an F-86 going close to 700 miles per hour, that distance is covered in 12 minutes.

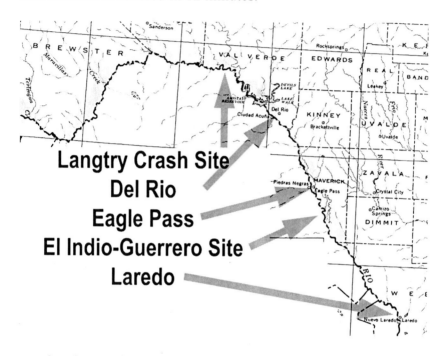

Langtry Crash Site
Del Rio
Eagle Pass
El Indio-Guerrero Site
Laredo

Condition of Crashed UFO

The *Eisenhower Briefing Document* describes the El Indio-Guerrero UFO as having been "almost totally incinerated." Such is not the case in Willingham's account of what he saw in Langtry. Willingham saw an object that was still intensely hot and that had expelled some debris during the crash, but it was not almost incinerated.

The DEW Line

Willingham has consistently stated that the UFO he encountered was first picked up by the Distant Early Warning (DEW) radar system in Canada. The first phase of the DEW did not become operational until 1952; therefore, Willingham's UFO encounter could not have occurred any earlier than 1952.

The B-52s

Willingham states that, on the day of his UFO encounter, he was part of a group of jets that were flying escort for B-47s and B-52s. He recalls that the B-52s were just being integrated into the military air arsenal. Since the first B-52s did not begin flying missions until late 1954 and early 1955, it is doubtful that Willingham's case could have taken place much prior to 1955, although there were B-52 prototypes being tested as early as 1951.

Dyess Air Force Base

In his 1977 NICAP affidavit, Willingham mentions flying over Dyess Air Force base in Abilene, Texas, shortly before the initial UFO sighting. The air base that became Dyess did not become operational until April 1956 and did not receive the name "Dyess" until eight months later. Willingham now says that his reference to Dyess was a memory lapse. He states that he was actually flying out of Carswell AFB in Fort Worth, Texas, and that he was flying in the vicinity of Goodfellow AFB in San Angelo when he first encountered the streaking UFO.

Conclusion

Willingham's story of a UFO crash near Del Rio was known to a small group of people as early as 1967, when the tale appeared in a Pennsylvania newspaper of limited circulation. The *Eisenhower Briefing Document* story about a crash at El Indio-Guerrero, for which no eyewitnesses have surfaced, was not disclosed until 1984.

Robert B. Willingham, July 2007 (Photo by Noe Torres)

Robert Willingham has been called a "credible witness" by a number of key UFO researchers, including Todd Zechel, Bruce Maccabee, and Ryan S. Wood. Although none of the other eye-witnesses in Willingham's case have spoken publicly, there do appear to have been quite a number of other witnesses, including:

1) Jack Perkins, the electrical engineer who visited the crash site with Willingham [Perkins died approximately 2001].

2) The pilots of three other F-86 Sabres (including George Smithson) who were in the air alongside Willingham's plane when the initial sighting was made,

3) The pilot and crewmembers of the B-47 that the F-86s were escorting.

4) About 30 Mexican soldiers and 15-20 Mexican officers and "government officials."

5) The Air Force or intelligence forces that arrived at the crash site and removed all debris after Willingham left.

Todd Zechel, the first UFO researcher to interview Willingham, said, "It became clear he was unsure of the date or location of the supposed crashed saucer event." Willingham now admits that he was having trouble getting his thoughts in order due to the effects of the head injury he sustained in Korea, but he insists that the story as told in this book is accurate to the best of his knowledge.

Willingham also admits some hesitation and reservations when Zechel urged him to give a written affidavit to NICAP in 1977. The statement he ended up filing was extremely brief, gave no date, excluded important information, and included a couple of factual errors.

Willingham also admits that when he first came forward with his story, he requested to be identified as "Burton Willingham," hoping to maintain some small measure of anonymity and, perhaps, of deniability. In military records, he was known as "Robert B. Willingham."

What follows is the NICAP affidavit filed in 1977 by Willingham:

"Down in Dyess Air Force Base in Texas *[He now states that he was actually flying out of Carswell AFB in Fort Worth and was in the vicinity of Goodfellow AFB, San Angelo, when he first saw the UFO]*, we were testing what turned out to be the F-94 *[Although he did fly F-94s during this era, he now states that he was piloting an F-86 on the day of this incident]*. They reported on the scope that they had an unidentified flying object at a high speed going to intercept our course. It became visible to us and we wanted to take off after it. Headquarters wouldn't let us go after it and we played around a little bit. We got to watching how it made 90 degree turns at this high speed and everything. We knew it wasn't a missile of any type. So then, we confirmed it with the radar control station on the DEW line, and they kept following it and they claimed that it crashed somewhere off between Texas and the Mexico border.

"We got a light aircraft, me and my copilot *[His co-pilot on the Aeronca was an electrical engineer named Jack Perkins]*, and we went down to the site. We landed out in the pasture right across from where it hit. We got over there. They told us to leave and everything else, and then armed guards came out, and they started to form a line around the area. So, on the way back *[to the Aeronca]*, I saw a little piece of metal so I picked it up and brought it back with me. There were two sand mounds that came down and it looked to me like this thing crashed right between them. But it went into the ground, according to the way people were acting around it. So we never did get up to the site to see what had crashed *[He now says that he walked up to within 35 feet of the object]*. But you could see for, oh I'd say, three to five hundred yards where it went across the sand.

"It looked to me, I guess from the metal that we found, that it either had a little explosion or it began to disintegrate. Something caused this metal to come apart.

"It looked like something that was made because it was honeycombed. You know how you would make a metal that would cool faster. In a way it looked like magnesium steel but it had a lot of carbon in it. I tried to heat it with a cutting torch. It just wouldn't melt. A cutting torch burns anywhere from 3200 to 3800 degrees Fahrenheit and it would make the metal hot but it wouldn't even start the metal to yield."

It is certainly possible that, due to the threats made against him, Willingham was unprepared to fully reveal the truth and that, consequently, he was deliberately vague in his statements and perhaps even occasionally misleading. "But now I'm 82 years old," he told the authors. "If I want to talk about it, I'll talk about it."

Because he did not give many specific details until recently, a number of UFO researchers took his 1977 NICAP affidavit and came up with their own "versions" of Willingham's story, filling in the gaps with speculation and, in some cases, outright deception. Willingham's brief NICAP statement has been torn apart phrase by phrase for thirty years, although few researchers have ever bothered to seek him out for answers to the questions that are not answered by the affidavit.

Although Willingham was never asked, some UFO researchers, it seems, decided that December 6, 1950 was the date that fit best for the Willingham case. Despite the fact that Willingham was serving in Korea at the time, the1950 date was very desirable to UFO investigators for two reasons:

1)   Documents exist proving that the U.S. military had gone into a "high alert" status on December 6, 1950, due to the sighting of unidentified flying objects in the northeastern U.S. An FBI memo, along with statements from President Harry S. Truman and others, establish the date as a significant UFO-related event.

2)   Once the Eisenhower Briefing Document surfaced in 1984, December 6, 1950 became significant, because it is mentioned in the document as the date of a UFO crash about 75 miles south of Del Rio.

For UFO researchers, having these three dots connected gives them a nice, tidy package, and, as of the writing of this book, the Willingham story appears in numerous books and on several Web sites with a December 6, 1950 date and with subtle suggestions that the crash retrieval happened near El Indio-Guerrero. The only problem is that Robert Willingham never said it happened in 1950; in fact, it could not have happened in 1950. Second, he never said it happened in the El Indio-Guerrero area; rather, he has always identified the crash site as being at Langtry, Texas.

19

WILLINGHAM & THE *KECKSBURG* CASE

After 1964, although he no longer worked with *Project Blue Book*, Willingham maintained a strong interest in UFOs, and when presented with the opportunity, he was always eager to do a little investigating on his own. One such opportunity came on December 9, 1965, while living in the Harrisburg, Pennsylvania area, about a two-and-a-half hour drive from the small town of Kecksburg.

Pennsylvania Highway Map Showing Kecksburg

"I just went out there by myself to see what it was and look it over. There was a lot of military activity in the area. I went up to this one place, and the guards wouldn't let me in, so I went down to another spot. Gosh, the woods were full of people, slipping in there."

Willingham heard about the incident from one of his fellow Air Force reservists in Harrisburg. "One of the guys who was flying at that time reported it in to all pilots," He remembers. "It came through our headquarters to the reserves and to all pilots. They said they had a bright, orange-looking light that crashed in that certain area and to stay clear. And they gave the coordinates and all that."

The Great Lakes Fireball and Kecksburg Incident

There is some speculation that the reentry of the Cosmos 96/Venera-type spacecraft was responsible for a fireball which was seen over southwestern Ontario, Canada and at least eight states from Michigan to New York at 4:43 p.m. EST (21:43 UT) on 9 December 1965. Investigations of photographs and sightings of the fireball indicated its path through the atmosphere was probably too steep to be consistent with a spacecraft re-entering from Earth orbit and was more likely a meteor in a prograde orbit from the vicinity of the asteroid belt, and probably ended its flight over western Lake Erie. U.S. Air Force tracking data on Cosmos 96 also indicate the spacecraft orbit decayed earlier than 21:43 UT on 9 December. Other unconfirmed reports state the fireball subsequently landed in Pennsylvania southeast of Pittsburgh near the town of Kecksburg (40.2 N, 79.5 W) at 4:46 p.m. EST (although it should be noted that estimating the impact point of fireballs from eyewitness accounts is notoriously inaccurate). Uncertainties in the orbital information and reentry coordinates and time make it difficult to determine definitively if the fireball could have been the Cosmos 96 spacecraft.

Excerpt from Official NASA Report (NSSDC ID: 1965-094A)

The Kecksburg Incident, as it has come to be known, began on the afternoon of December 9, 1965, when a fiery object was seen streaking over Ontario, Canada and then across the skies of eight states in the northeastern United States before crashing

160

about 35 miles southeast of Pittsburgh, Pennsylvania. The National Aeronautics and Space Administration (NASA) first speculated that the fireball was a Russian-made Cosmos 96/Venera unmanned Venus lander but later admitted that the object's steep trajectory through the Earth's atmosphere probably ruled out that theory.

RESIDENT TELLS OF MYSTERIOUS INCIDENT—

Unidentified Flying Object Report Touches Off Probe Near Kecksburg

Greensburg (PA) Tribune-Review, Dec. 10, 1965, Page 1

While attempts began right away to explain the event away as either a meteorite or a fallen Russian spacecraft, a number of people in the Kecksburg area were convinced it was something else altogether. "Eyewitnesses in the small village of Kecksburg, about 30 miles southeast of Pittsburgh, claimed something crashed in the woods. A boy said he saw the object land; his mother saw a wisp of blue smoke arising from the woods and alerted authorities. Others from Kecksburg, including local volunteer fire department members, reported finding an object in the shape of an acorn and about as large as a Volkswagen Beetle. Writing resembling Egyptian hieroglyphics was also said to be in a band around the base of the object. Witnesses further reported that intense military presence, most notably Army, secured the area, ordered civilians out, and then removed the object on a flatbed truck. At the time, however, the military claimed they searched the woods and found 'absolutely nothing'" (*Wikipedia*, 1-4-2008).

Although his involvement in the Kecksburg case was minimal, Colonel Robert Willingham felt compelled to go to the scene of the crash and experience it for himself. Recalling memories of his own encounter with a crashed UFO, Willingham joined the throng of people walking around in the woods around Kecksburg trying to get a glimpse of the mysterious object.

On the following day, the regional newspaper, the *Greensburg Tribune-Review*, screamed the headline, "Unidentified Flying Object Report Touches Off Probe Near Kecksburg." The frontpage article written by Bob Gatty read as follows:

An eight-year-old boy, his mother, the Pennsylvania State Police and the military all added up to mystery Thursday night and early Friday morning in a wooded area near Kecksburg in Westmoreland County.

It all started when an unidentified flying object (UFO) was reported sighted by the son of Mr. and Mrs. Arnold Kalp of Acme RD 1.

"Nevin saw it first," Mrs. Kalp told me as we stood along a dirt road near the woods where State Police and Army officials apparently were searching for an "object."

"He said it looked like a flaming star. It left a trail of flames behind it and fell in the woods," she added, pointing to the spot where her son said the UFO had fallen.

"Then I came out to look and I saw some smoke. Then it turned sort of cloudy, and went away almost like it buried itself in the ground."

Mrs. Kalp's story was told to me and other reporters more than five hours after the first report of the UFO was received.

After she saw the smoke, about 4:45 p.m., she heard a radio report that said an airplane has possibly crashed into the woods. So, Mrs. Kalp explained, she phoned the radio station to report that no plane had fallen, just the fireball.

Mrs. Kalp told reporters that she had been told by a Navy officer not to "tell anyone where it happened" until the area was sealed and an investigation begun.

"I never received so many phone calls in my whole life," she said. "Finally I just let it ring, then lifted up the receiver and put it back down. The state police had to clear the line to talk to me."

When I arrived near the scene of the sighting with Photographer Jim Downs, we were denied entrance to the road leading to the area where the UFO had reportedly fallen.

"We've been ordered by the state police and the army not to let anybody in," explained Dale Howard, a Kecksburg volunteer fire policeman.

Then, while at Howard's home using the telephone, Jim Mayes of Mammoth walked in and said he and six other fellows had seen three blue flashing lights near the area of the earlier sighting.

We went into the field (Downs and I) with Mayes and Howard to look for the lights. There were none.

Then the state police returned along with military officials. This time they went into the woods from the field where we had searched, apparently looking for the UFO.

A state trooper apparently assigned to handle the huge crowd that had formed then reported that "all search results are negative as far as we know, there's nothing there so far."

He said officers had left earlier "because we were satisfied that nothing was there. We returned because somebody reported seeing three huge flashing lights in the area."

As for Howard, who lives about a mile from the scene, he said he did not see the UFO, but felt the impact. "It caused a vibration here at home," he told me. "It hit with a big thump."

The last search party, which included three military men and State Police Fire Marshal Carl Metz, could be seen from the road where we stood, searching the area with flashlights.

Clearly, the Kecksburg case caused Willingham to reexamine the memories of his own UFO crash experience. After the Kecksburg incident, the public's interest in UFOs skyrocketed in Pennsylvania, and numerous UFO sightings continued throughout the state. Some of the sightings were reported by members of the Civil Air Patrol, of which Willingham was a part. Two years after Kecksburg, a reporter for a weekly newspaper in Mechanicsburg, Pennsylvania, was following up on UFO sightings made by the Civil Air Patrol, and he talked to Willingham, who told him, "Well, I once saw one of these things crash down on the Mexican border."

The resulting newspaper article in 1967 represented Willingham's first public disclosure about his incredible experience, and it eventually led to his NICAP disclosure in 1977 and the television documentary by Japan TV in 1978. Although overshadowed by the mania surrounding 1980's *The Roswell Incident* by Charles Berlitz and William Moore, Willingham's story nonetheless remains every bit as intriguing and riveting as the revelations about the 1947 New Mexico UFO crash.

20

THE COLONEL'S WISDOM

In the many hours spent by the authors interviewing Colonel Robert B. Willingham for this book, his candor and sincerity were strongly evident. During visits to his home in North Texas, he went out of his way to treat us with great courtesy and hospitality. Despite many years of being hounded by sometimes-unscrupulous reporters regarding the 1977 NICAP report about his UFO encounter, he retains a wonderful attitude and sense of humor.

Colonel Willingham (left) with Author Noe Torres, March 2008

165

At age 82, the colonel has achieved a lifestyle of comfortable satisfaction with the way things are. Even so, he is not happy to be just an observer of life, but remains a very active participant in it. He plays guitar in a musical group called the *Texas Rough-necks*, which performs regularly in the town square and at other local venues. As a highly experienced ham radio operator, he actively assists with emergency preparedness when serious weather or other dangerous situations threaten the Archer County area.

Walking around town with him, it quickly becomes clear that he is known and admired by everyone in the tiny community where he lives. As we walked around downtown, everyone we encountered stopped to greet or talk with him, people in passing cars waved, and even children and teenagers acknowledged him. "Well, it's a very small town," Willingham says with a grin.

"I lived many years in Pennsylvania, but I got tired of the traffic and the congestion," he says, as he surveys the few busi-nesses that remain open in the center of town. "So, I came back here to Texas, where I was born and raised."

The Colonel Smiles during an Interview at His Home, July 2007

During one of our interview sessions, I expressed admiration at his many accomplishments, including serving under General George S. Patton during World War II, helping prepare the way for Normandy, becoming one of the first jet fighter pilots, receiving a purple heart in Korea, flying numerous Cold War jets, rising to the rank of a full colonel in the Air Force Reserve, and so on. He listened intently to the recitation of honors, and, with a gleam in his eye and a smile, replied, "Well, you know, I got in the military because there just wasn't that much else for me to do back then."

Willingham (left) With Author Ruben Uriarte, March 2008

Here is a truly remarkable, humble human being, who accomplished what he did by sheer grit and spirited determination. He does not come from a privileged background and was not part of any inner circle during his time in the military. Perhaps that helps to explain why he, unlike so many others, was willing to speak up about what he saw. He truly fits the description of a rugged individualist, a self-made man, and, he is also very much of a free spirit. Here is a person who calls a spade a spade. There is simply no deception in him. It takes no more than five minutes of speaking with him before one becomes convinced that there is no chance his UFO story is made up.

His entire encounter, from the time he first saw the UFO streaking across the Texas sky to the time he was forced to leave the scene of the UFO crash, occurred over a period of just a few hours. He spent no more than thirty minutes at the scene of the crash. The whole experience encompasses just one solitary day in a long, full life of 82 years. "Remember, I'm talking about something that happened over 50 years ago," he told us. "It was also something that I was forced to put out of my mind for many years before I finally decided to talk about it."

Willingham in 2004 Photo

He has never sought to profit from his experience, nor has he ever sought out publicity. People have had to coax information out of him, a little at a time over the years. "It was just something that happened that one day, and that was it." He admits it was a memorable event and a very puzzling one, but it was only one day of his life.

Robert Willingham is a man who is intensely proud of his military service to America. Despite the fact that he was bullied by some in the military about his UFO encounter and may have even lost his pension over it, he remains a true and faithful patriot. He is satisfied to play out whatever hand is dealt to him.

Although he still suffers greatly from the effects of the combat injuries he sustained in Korea, he remains positive and upbeat. He drives himself to his medical appointments and scheduled surgeries, adopting the attitude of taking each day as it comes and making the most of his remaining time on earth.

After our first visit to his home in 2007 was over and it was time for us to leave him, the colonel offered to show us a better route for returning to our hotel in Dallas. We followed him to a convenience store near his home, and then, looking over the map of North Texas spread out on our hood, he suggested a route that would save us a good amount of time in our return to Dallas.

"I've traveled all these roads many times," he added, rubbing his chin. "After living here for so long, you don't like to take the same route every time – so I vary it. But, this way I'm showing you is definitely the most direct way."

He smiled as we nodded in agreement and folded up the map. "You have a great trip, and come back to visit again real soon," he smiled.

And, when we went our separate ways, we felt overwhelmed by the feeling that we were honored to have met such a truly remarkable man. Maybe the UFO experience is a mechanism of fate by which Robert Willingham will finally receive long-overdue recognition for his faithful and honorable service to his country.

EPILOGUE:
AN APPEAL TO OUR READERS

Although the events described in this book occurred many decades ago, the authors are certain that more information about the case is yet to come to light. Members of the armed forces who served with Colonel Willingham, or perhaps their children or grandchildren, may have heard snippets of this fascinating story. Persons may yet come forward who many years ago heard in hushed whispers the story of a UFO crash along the Texas-Mexico border in the 1950s. We, the authors, invite any reader who has more information about this case to please contact us through the publisher of our book or by visiting our Web site: *www.roswellbooks.com*. Anyone disclosing information about this case may remain completely anonymous.

Among persons who may hold valuable information that will further unlock this tremendous mystery are the following:

1) Willingham's fellow F-86 pilots from Carswell Air Force Base in the mid-1950s, including George Smithson, or their descendents.

2) The pilot and crewmembers of the B-47 that the F-86s were escorting on the day of the UFO encounter, or their families.

3) The family of the late Jack Perkins, the electrical engineer who visited the crash site with Willingham,

4) The Mexican Army personnel and other "government officials" who saw the crashed UFO across the Rio Grande River from Langtry, Texas.

5) The descendants of the unnamed individual who "paddled" across the river from Langtry and talked to Willingham about seeing the UFO crash.

6) The Air Force or intelligence forces that arrived at the crash site and removed all debris after Willingham left.

7)   The Marine Corps major and other metallurgy lab personnel who saw and handled the UFO fragment recovered by Willingham.

8)   The military intelligence personnel who threatened Willingham, warning him never to speak about his UFO sighting.

9)   Others in the military who saw accounts of the Willingham case cross their desk or who otherwise learned about the incident.

In his autobiography *Leap of Faith*, astronaut L. Gordon Cooper wrote, "I don't believe in fairy tales, but when I got into flying and military aviation, I heard other pilots describe too many unexplained examples of UFOs sighted around Earth to rule out the possibility that some forms of life exist beyond our own world."

"I knew the government was keeping a lot of secrets when it came to UFOs…. From my association with aviation and space, I had a pretty good idea of what kinds of craft existed on this planet and their performance capabilities. I believed that at least some of the UFOs – the truly unexplained ones – could be from another technologically advanced civilization, and I wasn't afraid to say so."

We appeal to you, our readers, if you have any information pertaining to the Willingham case, or other similar cases, please contact us through our publisher or our Web site, *www.roswellbooks.com.* The truth remains elusive, and yet it has surely gotten closer, if only by small degrees, in the last few years.

SPECIAL THANKS

The authors thank all the wonderful people who have supported our endeavors, including Dr. Bruce Maccabee, Stanton Friedman, Julie Schuster and the entire staff of the Roswell UFO Museum, Captain Mark Uriarte (U.S. Air Force, Ret.), Jim Castle of Castle Digital Design, Captain Jack of Paranormal Radio, Steve Andrasko, Robin Torres, Stephen Torres, Pike & Joyce Murphy, Patrick Richards, Elaine Douglass, and many, many others.

Special Thanks to the Fine People of Roswell, New Mexico, Because of You, Stephen Loves ET.

APPENDIX

TOP SECRET / MAJIC
EYES ONLY
NATIONAL SECURITY INFORMATION

```
••••••••••••••
•  TOP SECRET  •
••••••••••••••
```

EYES ONLY   COPY ONE OF ONE.

BRIEFING DOCUMENT: OPERATION MAJESTIC 12

PREPARED FOR PRESIDENT-ELECT DWIGHT D. EISENHOWER: (EYES ONLY)

18 NOVEMBER, 1952

WARNING: This is a TOP SECRET - EYES ONLY document containing compartmentalized information essential to the national security of the United States. EYES ONLY ACCESS to the material herein is strictly limited to those possessing Majestic-12 clearance level. Reproduction in any form or the taking of written or mechanically transcribed notes is strictly forbidden.

```
••••••••••••••
  TOP SECRET
```

TOP SECRET / MAJIC   T52-EXEMPT (E)
EYES ONLY   EYES ONLY   (1-1)

The Eisenhower Briefing Document

TOP SECRET / MAJIC

EYES ONLY

* TOP SECRET *
....

EYES ONLY

COPY ONE OF ONE.

SUBJECT: OPERATION MAJESTIC-12 PRELIMINARY BRIEFING FOR
    PRESIDENT-ELECT EISENHOWER.

DOCUMENT PREPARED 18 NOVEMBER, 1952.

BRIEFING OFFICER: ADM. ROSCOE H. HILLENKOETTER (MJ-1)

NOTE: This document has been prepared as a preliminary briefing
only. It should be regarded as introductory to a full operations
briefing intended to follow.

. . . . . .

OPERATION MAJESTIC-12 is a TOP SECRET Research and Development/
Intelligence operation responsible directly and only to the
President of the United States. Operations of the project are
carried out under control of the Majestic-12 (Majic-12) Group
which was established by special classified executive order of
President Truman on 24 September, 1947, upon recommendation by
Dr. Vannevar Bush and Secretary James Forrestal. (See Attachment
"A".) Members of the Majestic-12 Group were designated as follows:

    Adm. Roscoe H. Hillenkoetter
    Dr. Vannevar Bush
    Secy. James V. Forrestal*
    Gen. Nathan F. Twining
    Gen. Hoyt S. Vandenberg
    Dr. Detlev Bronk
    Dr. Jerome Hunsaker
    Mr. Sidney W. Souers
    Mr. Gordon Gray
    Dr. Donald Menzel
    Gen. Robert M. Montague
    Dr. Lloyd V. Berkner

The death of Secretary Forrestal on 22 May, 1949, created
a vacancy which remained unfilled until 01 August, 1950, upon
which date Gen. Walter B. Smith was designated as permanent
replacement.

....
* TOP SECRET *

TOP SECRET / MAJIC

EYES ONLY

EYES ONLY

T52-EXEMPT (E)

002

EISENHOWER BRIEFING DOCUMENT

A-3

003

On 24 June, 1947, a civilian pilot flying over the Cascade
Mountains in the State of Washington observed nine flying
disc-shaped aircraft traveling in formation at a high rate
of speed. Although this was not the first known sighting
of such objects, it was the first to gain widespread attention
in the public media. Hundreds of reports of sightings of
similar objects followed. Many of these came from highly
credible military and civilian sources. These reports resulted in independent efforts by several different elements
of the military to ascertain the nature and purpose of these
objects in the interests of national defense. A number of
witnesses were interviewed and there were several unsuccessful
attempts to utilize aircraft in efforts to pursue reported
discs in flight. Public reaction bordered on near hysteria
at times.

In spite of these efforts, little of substance was learned
about the objects until a local rancher reported that one
had crashed in a remote region of New Mexico located approximately seventy-five miles northwest of Roswell Army Air
Base (now Walker Field).

On 07 July, 1947, a secret operation was begun to assure
recovery of the wreckage of this object for scientific study.
During the course of this operation, aerial reconnaissance
discovered that four small human-like beings had apparently
ejected from the craft at some point before it exploded.
These had fallen to earth about two miles east of the wreckage
site. All four were dead and badly decomposed due to action
by predators and exposure to the elements during the approximately one week time period which had elapsed before their
discovery. A special scientific team took charge of removing
these bodies for study. (See Attachment "C".) The wreckage
of the craft was also removed to several different locations.
(See Attachment "B".) Civilian and military witnesses in
the area were debriefed, and news reporters were given the
effective cover story that the object had been a misguided
weather research balloon.

003

175

TOP SECRET / MAJIC   004

EYES ONLY
* TOP SECRET *

EYES ONLY   COPY ONE OF ONE.

A covert analytical effort organized by Gen. Twining and
Dr. Bush acting on the direct orders of the President, resulted in a preliminary concensus (19 September, 1947) that
the disc was most likely a short range reconnaissance craft.
This conclusion was based for the most part on the craft's
size and the apparent lack of any identifiable provisioning.
(See Attachment "D".) A similar analysis of the four dead
occupants was arranged by Dr. Bronk. It was the tentative
conclusion of this group (30 November, 1947) that although
these creatures are human-like in appearance, the biological
and evolutionary processes responsible for their development
has apparently been quite different from those observed or
postulated in homo-sapiens. Dr. Bronk's team has suggested
the term "Extra-terrestrial Biological Entities", or "EBEs",
be adopted as the standard term of reference for these
creatures until such time as a more definitive designation
can be agreed upon.

Since it is virtually certain that these craft do not origin-
ate in any country on earth, considerable speculation has
centered around what their point of origin might be and how
they get here. Mars was and remains a possibility, although
some scientists, most notably Dr. Menzel, consider it more
likely that we are dealing with beings from another solar
system entirely.

Numerous examples of what appear to be a form of writing
were found in the wreckage. Efforts to decipher these have
remained largely unsuccessful. (See Attachment "E".)
Equally unsuccessful have been efforts to determine the
method of propulsion or the nature or method of transmission
of the power source involved. Research along these lines
has been complicated by the complete absence of identifiable
wings, propellers, jets, or other conventional methods of
propulsion and guidance, as well as a total lack of metallic
wiring, vacuum tubes, or similar recognizable electronic
components. (See Attachment "F".) It is assumed that the
propulsion unit was completely destroyed by the explosion
which caused the crash.

* TOP SECRET *

EYES ONLY TOP SECRET / MAJIC   T52-EXEMPT (E)

EYES ONLY   004

EISENHOWER BRIEFING DOCUMENT

. . . .
* TOP SECRET *
. . . .

COPY ONE OF ONE.

A need for as much additional information as possible about these craft, their performance characteristics and their purpose led to the undertaking known as U.S. Air Force Project SIGN in December, 1947. In order to preserve security, liason between SIGN and Majestic-12 was limited to two individuals within the Intelligence Division of Air Materiel Command whose role was to pass along certain types of information through channels. SIGN evolved into Project GRUDGE in December, 1948. The operation is currently being conducted under the code name BLUE BOOK, with liason maintained through the Air Force officer who is head of the project.

On 06 December, 1950, a second object, probably of similar origin, impacted the earth at high speed in the El Indio - Guerrero area of the Texas - Mexican boder after following a long trajectory through the atmosphere. By the time a search team arrived, what remained of the object had been almost totally incinerated. Such material as could be recovered was transported to the A.E.C. facility at Sandia, New Mexico, for study.

Implications for the National Security are of continuing importance in that the motives and ultimate intentions of these visitors remain completely unknown. In addition, a significant upsurge in the surveillance activity of these craft beginning in May and continuing through the autumn of this year has caused considerable concern that new developments may be imminent. It is for these reasons, as well as the obvious international and technological considerations and the ultimate need to avoid a public panic at all costs, that the Majestic-12 Group remains of the unanimous opinion that imposition of the strictest security precautions should continue without interruption into the new administration. At the same time, contingency plan MJ-1949-04P/78 (Top Secret - Eyes Only) should be held in continued readiness should the need to make a public announcement present itself. (See Attachment "G".)

. . . .
TOP SECRET MAJIC

EYES ONLY

T52-EXEMPT (E)

177

TOP SECRET / MAJIC
EYES ONLY

• • • • • • • • • • • • •
• TOP SECRET •
• • • • • • • • • • • •

EYES ONLY   COPY ONE OF ONE.

ENUMERATION OF ATTACHMENTS:

*ATTACHMENT "A".......Special Classified Executive
                     Order #092447. (TS/EO)

*ATTACHMENT "B".......Operation Majestic-12 Status
                     Report #1, Part A. 30 NOV '47.
                     (TS-MAJIC/EO)

*ATTACHMENT "C".......Operation Majestic-12 Status
                     Report #1, Part B. 30 NOV '47.
                     (TS-MAJIC/EO)

*ATTACHMENT "D".......Operation Majestic-12 Preliminary
                     Analytical Report. 19 SEP '47.
                     (TS-MAJIC/EO)

*ATTACHMENT "E".......Operation Majestic-12 Blue Team
                     Report #5. 30 JUN '52.
                     (TS-MAJIC/EO)

*ATTACHMENT "F".......Operation Majestic-12 Status
                     Report #2. 31 JAN '48.
                     (TS-MAJIC/EO)

*ATTACHMENT "G".......Operation Majestic-12 Contingency
                     Plan MJ-1949-04P/78: 31 JAN '49.
                     (TS-MAJIC/EO)

*ATTACHMENT "H".......Operation Majestic-12, Maps and
                     Photographs Folio (Extractions).
                     (TS-MAJIC/EO)

• • • • • • • • • • • • •
• TOP SECRET •
TOP SECRET / MAJIC
EYES ONLY   EYES ONLY   T52-EXEMPT (E)

A-8

TOP SECRET

EYES ONLY

THE WHITE HOUSE
WASHINGTON

008

September 24, 1947.

MEMORANDUM FOR THE SECRETARY OF DEFENSE

Dear Secretary Forrestal:

    As per our recent conversation on this matter,
you are hereby authorized to proceed with all due
speed and caution upon your undertaking. Hereafter
this matter shall be referred to only as Operation
Majestic Twelve.

    It continues to be my feeling that any future
considerations relative to the ultimate disposition
of this matter should rest solely with the Office
of the President following appropriate discussions
with yourself, Dr. Bush and the Director of Central
Intelligence.

Harry Truman

TOP SECRET
EYES ONLY

008

Note: The attachments were not included.

BIBLIOGRAPHY

"Air Force Order on 'Saucers' Cited." *The New York Times* 28

   Feb. 1960: 30. *ProQuest*. Historical Newspapers. 12 Feb.

   2006.

"Air Force Orders Jet Pilots to Shoot Down Flying Saucers If

   They Refuse to Land." *Post-Intelligencer* (Seattle, WA)

   29 July 1952: 1.

Allen, Don. "Re: AIR #1 Report - 1/10." *Skeptic Tank Text Ar-*

   chive File. Jan. 2006

   <http://www.skepticfiles.org/index.htm>.

Auldbridge, Larry. "Jets on 24-Hour Alert To Shoot Down 'Sau-*

   cers'." *San Francisco Examiner.* 29 July 1952.

Berliner, Don, and Stanton T. Friedman. *Crash At Corona: the*

   U.S. Military Retrieval and Cover-Up of a UFO. New

   York: Marlowe & Company, 1992.

Berlitz, Charles, and William L. Moore. *The Roswell Incident.*

   Berkeley Books: New York, 1980.

BIBLIOGRAPHY

Cekander, Larry. "Research Team Uncovers New UFO Scientific Evidence." *UFO Hard Evidence*. Jan. 2003 <http://www.ufohardevidence.com>.

Clark, Jerome. *The UFO Book*. Detroit: Visible Ink Press, 1998.

Clark, Jerome, and Nancy Pear. *Strange & Unexplained Happenings: When Nature Breaks the Rules of Science*. Vol. 1. New York: UXL, 1995.

Colloff, Pamela. "1948: Laredo, Texas (Close Encounters of the Lone Star Kind)." *Texas Monthly*. 28 Jan. 2006 <http://www.texasmonthly.com/ranch/ufo/laredo.php>.

Cooper, L. Gordon. *Leap of Faith: An Astronaut's Journey into the Unknown*. New York: HarperCollins, 2000.

Dobbs, Michael. "Into Thin Air." *The Washington Post* 26 Oct. 2003, sec. W: 4.

"Documents Dated 1948-1959." *Majestic Documents: Evidence We are Not Alone*. Jan. 2006 <http://www.majesticdocuments.com>.

Dolan, Richard M. "UFO Secrecy and the Death of the Republic." *Through the Keyhole*. 28 Feb. 2005. 24 Jan. 2006 <http://keyholepublishing.com>.

"Electronic Reading Room." *Central Intelligence Agency Freedom of Information Act Documents*. Central Intelligence Agency. Jan. 2006 <http://www.foia.cia.gov>.

"Flight to Sverdlovsk." *Time*. 16 May 1960. <www.time.com>.

Friedman, Stanton T. *Top Secret / Majic*. New York: Marlowe & Company, 1996.

Friedman, Stanton T. "UFOs No Security Threat?" *MUFON UFO Journal*. June 2005. 20-21.

Garwood, Darrell. "Jets Told to Shoot Down Flying Discs." *Herald-News*. (Fall River, MA) 29 July 1952: 1.

Greer, Stephen M. *Disclosure: Military and Government Witnesses Reveal the Greatest Secrets in Modern History*. Crozet, VA: Crossing Point, Inc., 2001.

Gross, Loren E. *UFOs: A History, Volume 5: January-March, 1950*. Fremont, California. 1983.

BIBLIOGRAPHY

Haines, Gerald K. "CIA's Role in the Study of UFOs, 1947-

    1990." *Central Intelligence Agency Unclassified Docu-*

    ments. 1 Nov. 1997. Central Intelligence Agency. 12 Feb.

    2006

    <http://www.cia.gov/csi/studies/97unclass/ufo.html>.

Hall, Richard. *The UFO Evidence, Volume 2: A Thirty Year Re-*

    port. Lanham, MD: Scarecrow Press, 2001. 133.

Handbook of Texas Online, The. Texas State Historical Associa-

    tion. Jan. 2006

    <http://www.tsha.utexas.edu/handbook/online/>.

Howe, Linda Moulton. *Secret Radar Stations in New Mexico,*

    Parts 1 & 2. 2000 <http://www.earthfiles.com>.

"Images and Photos on-Line." *U.S. Army Medical Department &*

    School Portal. United States Army. 24 Jan. 2006

    <http://www.cs.armedd.army.mil/history/pics.html>.

Kean, Leslie. "Project Moon Dust and Operation Blue Fly: The

    Retrieval of Objects of Unknown Origin." *Coalition for*

Freedom of Information. 2002. 11 July 2007

<http://freedomofinfo.org>.

Kissner, J. Andrew. *Peculiar Phenomenon: Early United States*

Efforts to Collect and Analyze Flying Discs. 1994

<http://www.earthfiles.com>.

"Laredo Texas - 3 November 1952." *Project Blue Book Archive.*

3 Nov. 1952. 28 Jan. 2006

<http://www.bluebookarchive.org>.

Maccabee, Bruce. "Dec 1950 Crash & Willingham." *UFO Up-*

dates. 19 Jan. 2001. 25 Jan. 2006

<http://www.virtuallystrange.net/ufo/updates/2001/jan/m

20-003.shtml>.

Maccabee, Bruce. "Del Rio 1950." Emails to the authors. Jan.

2007 to Mar. 2008.

Maccabee, Bruce. "Immediate Saucer Alert! the Mystery of De-

cember 6, 1950." *NICAP.* 21 Jan. 2006

<http://www.nicap.org/reports/rena4.htm>.

BIBLIOGRAPHY

Maccabee, Bruce. "Radar Inspired National Alert." *National Investigations Committee on Aerial Phenomena.* 22 Jan.
2006 <http://www.nicap.org/reports/rina2.htm>.

"Majestic 12." *Federal Bureau of Investigation Freedom of Information Privacy Act.* Federal Bureau of Investigation.
12 Feb. 2006
<http://foia.fbi.gov/foiaindex/majestic.htm>.

"Man Claims Metal Fragment Came From a UFO." *Above Top
Secret.* 2 Feb. 2008. <http://www.abovetopsecret.com>.

Marrs, Jim. *Alien Agenda: Investigating the Extraterrestrial
Presence Among Us.* New York: Harper Paperbacks,
1997.

McAndrew, James. "Report on Project Mogul: Synopsis of Bal-
loon Research Findings." *Muller's Group - Lawrence
Berkeley Laboratory.* 21 Sept. 1995. United States Air
Force. 14 Feb. 2006 <http://muller.lbl.gov>.

"Military Bases Suspected of UFO Activity." *Alien Astronomer.*

13 Jan. 2006

<http://www.geocities.com/Area51/Shadowlands/6583/>.

"Nation Urged Not to Shoot at 'Saucers.'" *Los Angeles Times* 30

July 1952: 1. *ProQuest.* Historical Newspapers. 24 July

2006.

Pearson, Drew. "Air Force Admission on Saucers." *Washington*

Post. 29 July 1952: 29. *ProQuest.* Historical Newspa-

pers. 24 July 2006.

"Perry-Castañeda Library Texas Maps." *The University of Texas*

At Austin General Libraries. The University of Texas at

Austin. <http://www.lib.utexas.edu/maps/texas.html>.

"Project 1947: A Ghost Rocket Chronology." *Project 1947.* Sign

Historical Group. <http://www.project1947.com>.

Project Blue Book Archive. <http://www.bluebookarchive.org>.

Randle, Kevin D., and Donald R. Schmitt. *The Truth About the*

UFO Crash At Roswell. New York: Avon Books, 1994.

BIBLIOGRAPHY

Randle, Kevin D., and Donald R. Schmitt. *UFO Crash at Roswell*. New York: Avon Books, 1991. 248-250.

Randle, Kevin D., and Russ Estes. *Spaceships of the Visitors: an Illustrated Guide to Alien Spacecraft*. New York: Simon & Schuster, 2000.

Randle, Kevin D. *Case MJ-12: the True Story Behind the Government's UFO Conspiracies*. New York: HarperTorch, 2002.

Randle, Kevin D. *Conspiracy of Silence*. New York: Avon Books, 1997.

Randle, Kevin D. *A History of UFO Crashes*. New York: Avon Books, 1995.

Randle, Kevin D. *Invasion Washington: UFOs Over the Capitol*. New York: HarperTorch, 2001.

Randles, Jenny, and Peter Hough. *The Complete Book of UFOs*. New York: Sterling Company, 1994.

Ray, Richard. "Del Rio UFO Crash." *The Tex-Files*. Dallas: KDFW-TV. 1999.

Ritchie, David. *The Definitive Guide to Unidentified Flying Objects and Related Phenomena*. New York: Facts on File, 1994. 56.

Rock, Steve. "Bob White Maintains 'Belief' in Extraterrestrial Object." *Kansas City Star (MO)*. 10 June 2004.

Scully, Frank. *Behind the Flying Saucers*. Popular Library, 1951.

Snell, Scott. "Investigation Shows No Link Between Saucer Crash Tale and 1950 UFO Report." *Skeptical Eye* 1999. 2 Apr. 2006 <http://www.ncas.org/eyes/SE-11.4.pdf>.

Sobel, Dava. "The Truth About Roswell - Alleged Crash of a UFO Near Roswell, NM, on Jun 25, 1947." *Omni* Fall 1995. *FindArticles*. LookSmart. 27 Jan. 2006.

Stacy, Dennis. "Crash At El Indio - Alleged UFO Crash in Mexico." *Omni* Mar. 1995. *FindArticles*. 22 June 2006.

Stringfield, Leonard H. *UFO Crash/Retrievals, Status Reports I-VII*. 1978-1984.

Story, Ronald D., ed. *The Encyclopedia of UFOs*. Garden City, NY: Dolphin Books, 1980.

BIBLIOGRAPHY

"Texas UFO Crash." Japanese television documentary. 1978.

"UFO Roundup: Volume 10, Number 7." *UFOInfo*. 16 Feb.

2005. 20 Apr. 2006.

<http://www.ufoinfo.com/roundup/v10/rnd1007.shtml>.

"UFO Updates." *VSN - the Virtually Strange Network*. Jan. 2006

<http://www.virtuallystrange.net/ufo/updates/2000/dec/m

13-019.shtml>.

"Unidentified Flying Objects." *Federal Bureau of Investigation*

Freedom of Information Privacy Act. Federal Bureau of

Investigation. Jan. 2006

<http://foia.fbi.gov/foiaindex/ufo.htm>.

"Unidentified Flying Objects Research Guide." *U.S. Naval His-

torical Center*. 7 Mar. 2002. United State Navy. Feb.

2006 <http://www.history.navy.mil/faqs/faq29-1.htm>.

USAF Museum. United States Air Force. Jan. 2006

<http://www.wpafb.af.mil/museum>.

"U.S. Air Force Comes to Town, The." *Del Rio Chamber of Commerce*. 22 Jan. 2006 <http://www.drchamber.com/live/history/usaf.php>.

Von Daniken, Erich. *Chariots of the Gods*. New York: Berkley Books, 1999.

Whitcomb, Randall. "Project Silverbug – The Avrocar." *Crystal Links*. 3 Feb. 2008 <http://www.crystallinks.com>.

Willingham, Robert B. Personal interviews with the authors in Wichita Falls, Texas. July 2007 and March 2008.

Willingham, Robert B. Telephone interviews. June 2007 through March 2008.

Wood, Ryan S. *Majic Eyes Only: Earth's Encounters with Extra-terrestrial Technology*. Broomfield, CO: Wood Enterprises, 2005. 95-184.

"World Air Forces: Mexico." *Aeroflight*. 17 Jan. 2001. 21 Jan. 2006 <http://www.aeroflight.co.uk/index.html>.

York, Warren. "UFO Update." *Internet Sacred Text Archive*. 26 Dec. 2005 <http://www.sacred-texts.com>.

INDEX

Printed in the United States
142734LV00001B/78/P

9 780981 75970